California Bar Examination

Essay Questions and Selected Answers

February 2014

The State Bar Of California
Committee of Bar Examiners/Office of Admissions

180 Howard Street • San Francisco, CA 94105-1639 • (415) 538-2300
845 S. Figueroa Street • Los Angeles, CA 90017-2515 • (213) 765-1500

ESSAY QUESTIONS AND SELECTED ANSWERS

FEBRUARY 2014

CALIFORNIA BAR EXAMINATION

This publication contains the six essay questions from the February 2014 California Bar Examination and two selected answers for each question.

The answers were assigned high grades and were written by applicants who passed the examination after one read. The answers were produced as submitted by the applicant, except that minor corrections in spelling and punctuation were made for ease in reading. They are reproduced here with the consent of the authors.

Question Number	Subject
1.	Professional Responsibility
2.	Community Property
3.	Civil Procedure
4.	Real Property
5.	Constitutional Law
6.	Remedies

ESSAY EXAMINATION INSTRUCTIONS

Your answer should demonstrate your ability to analyze the facts in the question, to tell the difference between material facts and immaterial facts, and to discern the points of law and fact upon which the case turns. Your answer should show that you know and understand the pertinent principles and theories of law, their qualifications and limitations, and their relationships to each other.

Your answer should evidence your ability to apply the law to the given facts and to reason in a logical, lawyer-like manner from the premises you adopt to a sound conclusion. Do not merely show that you remember legal principles. Instead, try to demonstrate your proficiency in using and applying them.

If your answer contains only a statement of your conclusions, you will receive little credit. State fully the reasons that support your conclusions, and discuss all points thoroughly.

Your answer should be complete, but you should not volunteer information or discuss legal doctrines that are not pertinent to the solution of the problem.

Unless a question expressly asks you to use California law, you should answer according to legal theories and principles of general application.

Question 1

Three months ago, Dave was arrested for the burglary of a shoe store after a forensic investigation by the police department identified him as the burglar. Patty, a prosecutor, brought burglary charges against him.

A week ago, Patty saw a press release that the police chief was planning to issue to the media. It stated that Dave was a "transient" and had been "arrested for burglary by Inspector Ing, who is known for his ability to apprehend guilty criminals."

Four days ago, Patty received a report from a federal agency stating that the police department's forensic investigation identifying Dave as the burglar was unreliable.

Three days ago, Patty announced "ready for trial" at a pretrial conference.

Yesterday, Patty learned that two eyewitnesses had identified Dave as the burglar. Because she did not intend to use evidence from the forensic investigation, she did not disclose the federal agency report to Dave's attorney. Dave's attorney has never asked her to provide discovery.

This morning, Patty called the judge who will be presiding over Dave's trial to reassure him that there is ample non-forensic evidence to convict Dave.

What ethical violations, if any, has Patty committed? Discuss.

Answer according to California and ABA authorities.

QUESTION 1: SELECTED ANSWER A

Prosecutors have numerous unique ethical duties as a consequence of their role as public representatives and their power to interfere in the liberty of private persons. In general, a prosecutor has a duty to seek justice, not to secure a conviction at any cost.

Press Release Suggesting That the Accused Is Guilty

A lawyer has a duty not to make any statements that she should reasonably expect to be publicly disseminated and that are substantially likely to prejudice a judicial proceeding. A prosecutor in particular must not broadcast or allow to be broadcast a statement that expresses an opinion regarding the guilt or innocence of a criminal defendant. If a prosecutor knows that an attorney or law enforcement agent under her oversight plans to make such a statement, the prosecutor must make reasonable efforts to prevent the statement from being issued.

Here, the chief of police planned to issue a statement declaring that Dave had been apprehended by a detective "who is known for his ability to apprehend guilty criminals." Patty saw this press release before it was issued and knew that the chief planned to issue it. She therefore should reasonably have expected that it would be publicly disseminated. Patty will likely argue that the statement does not pose any problems, because in it the police chief does not directly express an opinion that Dave is guilty (or innocent). This argument will likely fail. The police chief's statement announces that Detective Ing has a reputation for apprehending guilty parties, which suggests strongly that the chief believes that Dave in particular is guilty. Patty may also argue that she has no duty to prevent the statement because it is attributable to the chief, not to her. This argument will likely also fail. As a prosecutor, Patty has a duty to make reasonable efforts to prevent law enforcement from making public statements that will prejudice a proceeding in which she is counsel. The chief's planned statement suggests strongly that the chief believes that Dave is guilty. This statement would likely prejudice the public against Dave, perhaps making it more difficult to select an unbiased jury. Patty therefore had a duty to make reasonable efforts to prevent the statement from being made.

Patty may argue that the other portions of the press release are not objectionable. For instance, a prosecutor generally may announce the name of a criminal defendant, the fact of an arrest, and the nature of the charges. That the police chief planned to announce that a person named Dave was arrested for burglary is therefore consistent with Patty's duties with regard to trial publicity, as is the chief's statement that Dave is a "transient." However, the statement that Dave was arrested by a detective who is known for apprehending "guilty criminals" suggests an opinion as to Dave's guilt, and amounts to a violation.

Patty's failure to prevent the chief's statement that Dave was arrested by a detective known for apprehending "guilty criminals" after learning that he planned to make it was a violation of her duty to avoid public statements that may prejudice a proceeding.

Prosecution Despite Lack of Probable Cause

A prosecutor's duty to seek justice requires that she never pursue a charge that she knows is unsupported by probable cause. Probable cause exists when the facts known to the prosecutor are sufficient to allow a person of reasonable prudence and caution in the prosecutor's position to seriously entertain the possibility that the defendant is guilty of the crime charged.

Here, Patty will argue that she has probable cause to pursue Dave's burglary charge to trial. She will note that two eyewitnesses have identified Dave as the burglar, and eyewitness testimony is usually sufficient to make out a prima facie case against an accused. The State Bar would likely point out that Patty did not learn of the eyewitness testimony until yesterday. Before that time, the sole evidence on which the charge was based was the police department's investigation. Four days ago, however, before Patty learned of the eyewitnesses, a federal report revealed that the forensic investigation was unreliable. The State Bar will argue that, as of this time, Patty lacked probable cause because the sole evidence on which the charge was based had been revealed to be suspect. The State Bar would be correct. In the two days between receiving the federal report and learning of the eyewitnesses, Patty lacked sufficient facts as would justify a reasonable person in believing that Dave was guilty. Instead of continuing to pursue the charge, she should have conducted further investigation to learn whether Dave was likely to be responsible for the burglary charged. Patty may argue that the mere existence of a report calling into question the police department's investigation does not alone establish that the investigation was faulty. This is true, but it does not excuse her conduct. At minimum, the report called the investigation into question. Patty should have pursued that question rather than continuing to rely blindly on the forensic evidence.

Patty's continued pursuit of the burglary charge after receiving the federal report was likely a breach of her duty not to pursue a charge in the absence of probable cause.

Lack of Candor Before the Tribunal

A lawyer's duties to uphold the integrity of the profession and to avoid prejudicing the administration of justice require that she make no false statements to a court in the course of a proceeding. This duty applies to prosecutors as well as to all other lawyers.

Here, Patty announced ready for trial three days ago at a pretrial conference. The day before the conference, she had learned that the sole evidence on which the burglary charge was then based, the police department's forensic report, was unreliable. Rather than announce this fact to the court, however, she told the court that she was ready for trial. Patty may argue that this statement was not a misrepresentation. She may assert that she intended to proceed to trial on the forensic evidence despite the federal report, perhaps in the belief that the report was mistaken. Other facts in this case belie that assertion. After the pretrial conference, as soon as Patty learned that there were eyewitnesses to the charged crime, she abandoned the forensic evidence. This indicates that she understood that the forensic evidence had limited value, and suggests that Patty did not truly believe that she was "ready for trial" when this evidence was all that was available. On the other hand, if Patty did believe that the forensic evidence was sufficient to proceed to trial, this fact reinforces the conclusion above that Patty breached her duty not to pursue a charge in the absence of probable cause.

Patty likely did not believe that she was ready for trial when she announced as much to the court, a breach of her duty of candor. If she did believe that she was ready when the only evidence available was the unreliable forensic evidence, her announcement of readiness for trial is a breach of her duty not to pursue a charge in the absence of probable cause.

Failure To Disclose Exculpatory Evidence to the Defense

The Due Process Clause of the United States Constitution imposes a duty on every prosecutor to disclose to the defense material evidence favorable on the issues of guilt or punishment. Evidence is "material" if the prosecutor's timely disclosure raises a reasonable possibility that the outcome of the trial would be different than if the evidence had been withheld. The duty to disclose exists even if the defense makes no discovery requests. A prosecutor is responsible for violating this duty even if she did not act in bad faith.

Here, Patty received a report from a federal agency suggesting that the police department's forensic investigation was unreliable. This evidence is favorable to Dave because he can use it to show that the forensic evidence deserves little weight. Patty will argue that the report is not material because she intends to rely on eyewitnesses, and does not plan to introduce the forensic evidence at all. She will assert accordingly that the defense will not be able to use the report to affect the outcome because it does not address the reliability of the eyewitnesses' testimony. This argument will fail. The report allows the defense to attack the reliability of the police department's entire investigation. By demonstrating that the forensic investigation was inept, the defense will be able to suggest that the police handled the eyewitnesses ineptly as well. Because the defense can use the report to undermine the police department's investigation, a reasonable possibility exists that it could influence at least one juror to vote not guilty, calling for a mistrial. This is sufficient to give rise to a reasonable possibility that disclosure of the report could lead to a different outcome. Patty may also argue that she has no duty to disclose the report because the defense never asked for it. This argument will also fail. A prosecutor has a duty to disclose exculpatory evidence in her possession whether the defense asks for it or not.

Patty's failure to disclose the federal report is a breach of her duty to disclose exculpatory evidence to the defense.

Improper Ex Parte Contact with the Presiding Judge

A lawyer's duty of fair play to her opposing counsel requires that she not engage in any ex parte contact with a judge in order to influence the outcome of a proceeding.

Here, Patty called the presiding judge in Dave's trial to assure him that she has sufficient non-forensic evidence to prove the burglary charge. There is no indication that she announced to Dave's counsel that she intended to make this contact or that she invited Dave to speak with the judge at the same time. This was an improper ex parte contact. Moreover, it was likely intended to influence the judge in the proceedings. That Patty felt the need to reassure the judge that she need not rely on the forensic evidence suggests that she knew or suspected that the judge had misgivings about the forensic evidence. Her reassurance was likely intended to assuage those misgivings. Making this communication in the absence of opposing counsel was a violation of Patty's duty of fair play.

By contacting the presiding judge ex parte in an attempt to influence him regarding the strength of her case, Patty violated her duty of fair play to opposing counsel.

QUESTION 1: SELECTED ANSWER B

Patty's Ethical Violations

Attorneys have a duty to represent their clients with diligence, competence and zealous representation. The attorney must conform their conduct with their client, courts, opposing counsel and other parties within the rules under the Business and Professions code and Ethical codes of conduct. Generally, the ABA and California are the same but I will note when they are different.

Here, Patty as prosecuting attorney has a duty to zealously represent the state and conform her conduct with the professional rules and uphold the integrity of our legal system. Patty has potentially violated some of these rules which will each be discussed in turn below.

Statements to the Public/Media

Patty likely committed an ethical violation when she knew the police chief was planning to issue a press release to the media containing prejudicial statements about Dave that would adversely affect his right to a fair trial and impartial jury.

An attorney may not make extrajudicial statements that would inhibit a defendant's right to a fair trial. An attorney cannot make statements about a trial that would prevent the selection of an impartial jury or prejudice the defendant. It is important public policy that the community not be tainted by these statements to the media; otherwise a defendant will be unable to obtain a fair trial with an impartial jury. However, there are a few matters where an attorney may make a statement to the public such as any defenses to the crime charged and an attorney may respond to accusations by another attorney. In other words, the attorney can make statements in rebuttal of any prejudicial statements made by opposing counsel. Without allowing statements of rebuttal the jury selection would be tainted and prevent a fair trial for the defendant. Statements may also be made when the police are still conducting an investigation and are seeking help from the public. For instance, looking for witnesses or information regarding persons of interest or whereabouts.

Here, Patty is a prosecutor bringing burglary charges against Dave. Patty is arguably responsible for statements by the police chief as he is the head of the department leading the investigation of the crime for which she is prosecuting. Patty knew of extrajudicial statements before they were made by the police chief because she saw the press release a week ago. As such, Patty has a duty to prevent any extrajudicial statements to the press by the police chief that would adversely affect Dave's right to a fair trial. Furthermore, Patty had knowledge of these statements and she knew of their potential prejudicial effect on Dave the defendant. Dave's attorney may argue Patty knew the police chief's statement contained prejudicial statements about his client because she knew the police chief was going to call Dave a "transient". Dave's Attorney will argue by telling the public Dave is a transient will have a prejudicial effect on the public. The public may infer guilt upon Dave because traditionally in our society being a transient indicates a lack of money and provides motive to rob a shoe store. Patty will counter argue statements as to the potential motive of the criminal act is a permissible statement. Patty cannot argue as a defense these statements were not made in an ongoing effort to solve a crime or gain information from the public and are thus permissible. It is possible the disciplinary boards or the court may not find the "transient" statement to have been so prejudicial as to be an ethical violation by Patty.

The second statement made by the police chief was that Dave was "arrested for burglary by Inspector Ing, who is known for his ability to apprehend guilty criminals." While the first part of the statement announcing Dave was arrested for burglary by Inspector Ing does not appear prejudicial, the police chief crossed the line with the statement "known for his ability to apprehend guilty criminals." This statement would have an extremely prejudicial effect on the public at large because he is stating Detective Ing only arrests those who are guilty criminals. Dave's right to a fair trial and impartial jury are tainted by such statements because it is telling the public by inference of his arrest he is guilty. Again, as prosecuting attorney Patty had a duty to prevent the police chief from making prejudicial statements about Dave to the public because she had knowledge of his press release he was planning to issue.

In conclusion, it is likely Patty will be found in violation of the ethical code of conduct because she knew of the police chief's press release stating Dave was arrested by Detective known for apprehending guilty criminals.

Malicious Prosecution: Bringing Charges Without Probable Cause

Patty committed an ethical violation by bringing charges against a defendant without sufficient probable cause.

A prosecuting attorney has a duty to not bring malicious actions and may only bring charges supported by probable cause. If a prosecutor initially has probable cause to bring charges but later finds out there is no probable cause (lack of evidence, etc.) then the charges against the Defendant must be dropped. In order to have probable cause there must be facts sufficient to indicate the defendant committed a criminal act. The policy behind this rule is to uphold the integrity of our justice system by only prosecuting individuals when there are sufficient facts to constitute a cause of action. This rule also prevents undue costs and waste of the court's time.

Here, Patty has made an ethical violation because she proceeded with the charges against Dave even after she learned the forensic investigation identifying Dave as the burglar was unreliable. Patty only initially brought the charges against Dave because of the forensic investigation identifying him as the burglar. This was sufficient probable cause because there was evidence indicating Dave committed a criminal act of burglary upon the shoe store. Thus far Patty has not committed a violation for filing charges against Dave for the burglary. However, four days ago, Patty received a report from a federal agency stating that the police department's forensic investigation identifying Dave as the burglar was unreliable. This negates probable cause to arrest Dave because there does not appear to be any other evidence linking him to the shoe store burglary. Furthermore, it was a federal agency reporting to Patty that the investigation was unreliable. This should have been a clear indication to Patty that she did not have probable cause and thus charges against Dave should have been dropped. Patty committed a violation when three days later she announced "ready for trial" at a pretrial conference. There are no other facts to indicate Patty had any probable cause to link Dave to the burglary and thus she committed an ethical violation by bringing charges without probable cause.

In conclusion, Patty will be in violation of bringing charges against a defendant with lack of probable cause because she did not have any evidence linking Dave to the burglary and otherwise announced she was ready for trial.

Duty of Diligence and Competent Representation

Patty potentially committed a violation of diligent and competent representation when she knowingly carried out charges against Dave for burglary after learning she no longer had sufficient probable cause.

An attorney has a duty to competently and diligently represent a client with the required skill, knowledge and experience required for the matter.

Patty potentially violated her duty to represent the state diligently and competently because she did not drop the charges against Dave after a lack of probable cause. It can be argued it would have been diligent for Patty to drop the charges against Dave because once the jury is sworn in Dave cannot be charged again due to double jeopardy. If there was a lack of evidence it would have been prudent of Patty to drop the charges and await discovery of further evidence sufficient to support probable cause. This indicates a violation of her diligent and competent representation of the state (and essentially the shoe store) because she is prosecuting a defendant who may have committed the crime but will not be convicted due to a lack of evidence.

False Statement to the Court

Patty made a false statement to the court when she stated she was ready for trial at a pretrial conference but had insufficient probable cause to carry out the charges against Dave for burglary.

However, Patty will argue she did not commit a violation because she had probable cause when she learned that two eyewitnesses had identified Dave as the burglar. Patty will still be in violation because this information was obtained after she told the court she was "ready for trial" at a pre-trial conference. This may be considered a false statement to the court which is another violation of ethical conduct. By falsely telling the court she was ready for trial indicates she still had probable cause to charge Dave. However, Patty did not have sufficient probable cause at the pretrial conference because she received a report from a federal agency stating the forensic investigation identifying Dave as the burglar was unreliable. Again, no other evidence was apparent linking Dave to the shoe store burglary. Furthermore, Patty did not attempt to alert the court to this false statement and it was made knowingly because she knew the report made her forensic evidence unreliable. Thus, Patty made a false statement to the court when she told them she was ready for trial although she had lack of probable cause. By continuing trial this would result in a waste of the court's time and expenses of attorney fees upon the defendant not to mention the stress of facing criminal charges.

Although Patty will argue she had sufficient probable cause because she had two eyewitnesses to identify Dave as the burglar this evidence did not arise until after the statement was made to the court. Patty will not be able to retroactively rectify the fact she made a false statement to the court.

In conclusion, Patty made an ethical violation by giving the court a false statement that she announced she was ready for trial at a pretrial conference.

Disclosure of Evidence to Opposing Counsel

Patty will be in violation of providing exculpatory evidence when she did not disclose the federal agency's report to Dave's attorney.

A prosecuting attorney has a duty to turn over any evidence that is helpful to the defense even outside of discovery requests. This goes towards the policy of providing a defendant with a fair trial giving both parties the same evidence to use in arguing their case. A prosecutor has access to evidence and resources a defense attorney may not have, such as federal agency reports. An attorney who does not disclose such evidence will be found in violation of the codes of ethical conduct.

Here, Patty did not disclose the federal agency report to Dave's attorney. Dave's attorney is likely a public defender since Dave is a transient. The public defender's office may not have access to the federal agency report stating that the police department's forensic investigation identifying Dave as the burglar was unreliable. This evidence is beneficial and essential to Dave's case because it shows the prosecution has no probable cause to bring charges. Essentially the federal agency report making the evidence unreliable is a strong piece of evidence to argue Dave's innocence. Thus, as prosecutor Patty should have disclosed the evidence to Dave's attorney within a reasonable time of its discovery.

Patty will argue that she was not intending to use evidence from the forensic investigation so she did not disclose it to Dave's attorney. She will further argue that Dave's attorney has never asked her to provide discovery so she was not required to disclose the report and could not have committed an ethical violation where there was no duty to disclose. This defense will not stand because Patty as prosecutor had a duty to disclose the beneficial evidence to Dave's attorney of her own accord. Furthermore, Dave's attorney had no indication of knowledge of the report's existence so he would not have known to ask for it. Thus, Patty remains in violation although Dave's attorney never specifically asked for the document.

In conclusion, Patty committed an ethical violation when she did not disclose the federal agency report which was of benefit to Dave's attorney.

Attorney Work Product Doctrine

Patty will argue the federal agency report is attorney work product doctrine and thus cannot not be turned over to Dave's attorney because of privilege. However, it is likely Dave's attorney can show undue hardship without the production of the federal agency report and thus Patty must turn over the report or will be in violation.

An attorney's work product of their thoughts, opinions, legal conclusions, labor or investigation by an agent falls under privileged information and is not discoverable by opposing counsel. However, when an attorney can show (i) a substantial need for the information or document and (ii) an undue hardship (such as excessive costs) and inability to reproduce the same document the court may grant an exception this rule. In California, the attorney needs to show a reasonable and compelling reason for the need to disclose the evidence. However, the information must be redacted (blacked out, crossed out) of any conclusions, opinions, thoughts about the case made by the attorney to whom the document belongs. This ensures the attorney's thoughts and any privileged information between themself and a client remains undisclosed to the opposing counsel.

Here, Dave's attorney will argue there was a substantial need for the information because it is proof his client is being wrongly accused for the shoe store burglary. Furthermore, Dave's attorney will have to show an undue hardship in obtaining the federal agency report and show he does not have access or it would be a great expense to duplicate the report. If the court were to grant the request then Patty's opinions, thoughts or legal conclusions about the case must be redacted or crossed out, thus keeping Patty's privilege intact and preventing inadvertent disclosures of client communications or her own legal conclusions.

In conclusion, it is likely Dave will have access to the federal agency document and Patty cannot use it in defense of her ethical violation of non-disclosure.

Extrajudicial Statements to a Judge

Patty committed an ethical violation when she made an out-of-court statement without the presence of counsel regarding the trial to the presiding judge.

An attorney may not make extrajudicial statements to the presiding judge regarding the case matter (outside of logistical issues) without the presence of other counsel or their knowledge. This prevents a prejudicial effect on the judge who will be presiding over the case and protects the defendant's sixth amendment right to a fair trial.

Here, Patty called the judge who will be presiding over Dave's trial to reassure him that there is ample non-forensic evidence to convict Dave. This is a statement out of court because Patty called the judge by telephone. Furthermore, Patty's statement was made to the judge without the presence of Dave's attorney. Patty's statement to the judge was regarding a matter for trial when she was telling the judge about evidence not yet admitted or presented at trial. Patty also "reassured" the judge there was ample non-forensic evidence to "convict" Dave. This statement puts in the mind of the judge Dave is guilty. Dave may waive his right to a jury trial and have a bench trial where the judge decides whether or not he is convicted. Thus Patty has given the judge information about the evidence not yet presented at trial. This was a clear ethical violation by making a prejudicial statement to the judge presiding over the burglary case and outside the presence of Dave's attorney.

In conclusion, Patty committed an ethical violation when she gave prejudicial information outside of trial to the judge that there was ample non-forensic evidence to convict Dave.

Question 2

Hank and Wendy are residents of California. Hank is a teacher and Wendy is an accountant.

In 2008, Hank and Wendy married. After their wedding, Wendy's mother deeded them a house as joint tenants. They moved into the house and used their earnings to furnish it in a lavish style, including an antique mirror in the entryway. One day, Hank gave the mirror to a friend who had admired it on a visit to the house.

In 2012, Wendy purchased a small office building where she established her own accounting practice. She paid for the building with funds saved from her earnings during her marriage and took title in her name alone.

In 2013, Hank and Wendy separated. Hank told Wendy that the house was henceforth her separate property and she said, "O.K."

After the separation, Wendy's income from the accounting practice tripled and she remodeled the office building with her increased earnings. Without Hank's knowledge, she then sold the building to Bob, who did not know that she was married.

In 2014, Wendy initiated dissolution proceedings.

1. What are Wendy's rights, if any, as to the antique mirror? Discuss.

2. What are Hank's and Wendy's rights, if any, as to the following:

   a) The house? Discuss.

   b) The accounting practice? Discuss.

   c) The office building? Discuss.

Answer according to California law.

QUESTION 2: SELECTED ANSWER A

Community Property Generally

Since Hank and Wendy are residents of California, the law of California will be applied in their divorce proceeding. California is a community property (CP) state. The general presumption is that all property acquired by either spouse during the marriage, real or personal, is CP. On the other hand, all property that is acquired by gift, bequest, devise or descent is considered separate property (SP) of the spouse who received it. In this case, the ownership of each of the assets will depend on whether the CP presumption controls, or the actions of the parties or some other presumptions have changed the character of the property. Each asset will be discussed separately below.

The Mirror

The first issue is whether Wendy has any rights in the antique mirror that Hank gave away to his friend. In this case the mirror was acquired during the marriage, and was purchased using the earnings of both parties; therefore the mirror is considered CP. There are no facts to indicate that the parties changed the character of the mirror and therefore the CP presumption is controlling.

Gift To the Friend

The issue here is whether Hank has fully disposed of the mirror by giving it away to his friend. After 1-1-1975, both spouses to the marriage acquired the rights to equal management and control of the marital assets. Under the rules regarding the rights of equal management and control, one spouse may not make a gift of CP without the consent of the other spouse.

Here, Hank gave the friend the mirror, and there is no indication that he asked for Wendy's permission before doing so. Hank may argue that although spouses may not make gifts of CP without the other spouse's permission, the general rule is that the parties can dispose of personal property. On the other hand, the general rule is that spouses may not dispose of personal property without the consent of the other spouse, for less than fair market value. Here, the facts indicate that the parties decorated their house in a "lavish style" and that the mirror was an antique; therefore it is reasonable to assume that this antique mirror was fairly valuable. Since Hank merely gave the mirror to a friend, and received no consideration for the gift, he has breached his spousal fiduciary duty owed to Wendy. The gift to the friend was improper.

When one spouse makes an improper gift, the other spouse has a right to set aside the gift. In this case, if Wendy were trying to contest the gift during the marriage, she could set aside the entire gift. However, at divorce, a spouse only has a right to set aside one-half of the gift, because the parties each have a one-half interest in all CP. In this case, Wendy would be able to set aside one-half of the gift at divorce. Since the gift was of personal property and a mirror cannot be physically divided, the court will probably value the mirror and award Wendy one-half of its value through another source of money during the dissolution.

The House

Next, the court must determine how to characterize the house that was given to Wendy and Hank sometime after 2008. Since the parties were married in 2008 and the house was acquired afterwards, it is presumed to be CP. However, in this case, the house was received as a gift. The facts indicate that Wendy's mother deeded it to them as joint tenants. As discussed above, gifts during the marriage are considered to be SP of the spouse receiving the gift. In addition, when parties own property in Joint Tenancy, during the marriage it is classified as two SP halves. Therefore, during the marriage, this house would be considered two SP halves owned by each spouse.

Actions By the Parties

The issue here is whether the discussion between Hank and Wendy in 2013 changed the character of the house. Here, the facts indicate that Hank told Wendy that the house was "henceforth her SP" and that Wendy said "ok." This is an attempt at a transmutation. A transmutation is an action by the spouses to change the character of the property that the spouses already own.

Prior to 1985, transmutations could be of the most informal character, including orally. Here, there was an oral agreement to transfer the house to Wendy's SP at the couple's separation in 2013. If this was prior to 1985, this would be valid. However, modernly a transmutation is not valid unless it is in writing, indicates that there is a change in the character of the property, and is signed by the adversely affected party. In this case, Hank would be the adversely affected party because he would be abandoning his one-half interest in the property and giving it to Wendy. However, since there was no signed writing, this oral promise to change the character of the property to Wendy's SP is unenforceable.

Anti-Lucas Legislation

Since the transmutation was ineffective, the court must now determine how to divide the property at dissolution. Here, the property is held in joint tenancy, which is inconsistent with the basic CP presumption that all property acquired during the marriage is CP. However, under the Anti-Lucas Legislation, for purposes of dissolution only, all property held jointly is treated as CP. This presumption can only be overcome by a statement in the deed that the parties intend to hold title differently or a written companion agreement. In this case, the mother merely deeded the property to the spouses as a gift. It is unlikely that they literally intended for the property to be owned one-half by each of them as their SP. In addition, there is no written agreement indicating otherwise. Therefore, the house will be treated as CP. Since the house is treated as CP at dissolution, both Hank and Wendy have a one-half interest in the property.

The general rule is that at divorce, CP should be divided equally in kind. However, the court can fashion other relief if necessary. In this case, since Hank evidenced an intent to give the house to Wendy, the court may allow Wendy to keep the house, and just award Hank the value of one-half of the house.

The Accounting Practice

Next, the court will address the accounting practice of Wendy's. Although Wendy was an accountant prior to the marriage, the facts indicate that she established her own practice in 2012 during the marriage. Since the work of a spouse is considered CP labor, the earnings a spouse earns from work are CP funds.

Calculating the Value Of the Business

When there is a spouse that has a SP business, the court must determine how to allocate the business and the earnings from the business. The court does this by applying one of two formulas, each of which will be discussed below.

Pereira

Under the Pereira formula, the court takes the initial investment of the spouse, multiplies it by a simple and arbitrary interest rate (typically 10%) and then multiplies that by the number of years the spouse worked in the business during the marriage. That figure is considered to be a rate of return on the initial investment, and is awarded to the spouse who started the business with her SP, the remaining amount is considered CP.

Van Camp

Under the Van Camp formula, the court will calculate a reasonable rate of earnings for the working spouse, and multiply that by the number of years the spouse worked during the marriage. This figure would then be awarded to the community as CP. The remaining funds would be considered SP of the spouse, and attributable to standard increases in value to the business due to the market.

In general, the court will use the Pereira formula when the increased value of the business was attributable to the work of the spouse in the business. In contrast, the courts will use Van Camp when the increase in value of the business is due to the overall market economy.

In this case, however, it does not appear that the court would use either approach. The facts indicate that the business was opened during the marriage, using money that Wendy had earned during the marriage. Because the money was earned during the marriage, the business itself is considered CP and not Wendy's SP. Therefore, the accounting business as of 2013 should be considered CP and should be divided equally between the parties at dissolution.

Post-Separation Earnings

In this case, the facts indicate that the earnings of the accounting practice tripled after the separation. The general rule is that marital community ends when there is physical separation of the parties with no intent to rekindle the relationship. Here, the facts indicate that the parties separated in 2013. It is unclear whether there was physical separation, but since Hank told Wendy that the house was her SP, it is likely that he moved out of the house at that time. If the court finds that 2013 was the date the marital community ended, then no CP could be established after that time, and all of the increased earnings in the accounting practice would be Wendy's SP. If the court finds that there was no true separation until 2014 when Wendy filed for divorce, then the accounting practice value as of 2014 would be divided equally between the parties as CP earned during the marriage. But, under these facts, it is most likely that the court will find that 2013 was the date that the marital community ended, and award the increased profits to Wendy as her SP.

The Office Building

Last, the court must determine the character of the office building in order to determine if Hank has any interest in it, notwithstanding the fact that Wendy sold it to Bob.

The property was acquired during the marriage using funds from Wendy's earnings; therefore the office building is initially characterized as CP.

<u>Actions Of the Parties</u>

The issue here is whether the general CP presumption can be rebutted since Wendy took title to the property in her name alone. Under California law, there is a form of the title presumption, which holds that the holder of record title to a property is presumed to be the true owner. In this case, Wendy will argue that the property is hers because she took title in her name alone, and therefore the form of the title prevails.

However, in order for the form of the title presumption to apply, the title must itself have evidentiary value. In this case, the title may not prevail, because there are no facts to indicate that Hank agreed to her taking title in her name alone. Wendy may argue that since the office was purchased with CP earnings, the community made a gift to her and she could take the property as her SP. However, there are no facts to support this. There is no evidence to show that Hank knew that she took title in her name alone, let alone that he agreed for her to do so. Therefore, the title will not be controlling. Since the property was acquired with CP funds, the property will be considered CP.

<u>Post 2013 Actions</u>

Although the property will be classified as CP, the court must determine how to handle the fact that Wendy remodeled the business with her increased earnings after the date of separation. As discussed above, all property that is acquired after the date of separation is considered to be SP of the acquiring spouse. In this case, Wendy's earnings from her accounting practice post 2013 are characterized as her SP.

SP Improvements To CP

Since the money used in the remodel was Wendy's SP, the court will treat this as a SP improvement to a CP asset. Historically, if a spouse contributed SP to a CP asset, it was considered a gift. However, modernly the general rule is that if a spouse contributes SP to a CP asset, he can be reimbursed for SP down payments, loan reductions, and improvements. Here, Wendy remodeled the office building and therefore this will be characterized as an improvement. Wendy will then be entitled to reimbursement to her SP for either the cost of the improvement, or the increased value to the building because of the improvement.

The Sale to Bob

In this case, the classification of the office building is slightly complicated by the fact that Wendy sold the property to Bob. The general rule is that when disposing of CP real property, both spouses must participate in the sale and sign the appropriate documents. However, in this case, the facts indicate that Wendy sold the house without Hank's knowledge, which means he clearly did not participate in the sale. Here, it was easier for Wendy to do this, because the house was titled in her name alone and therefore Bob was unaware that she was married.

When a spouse disposes of real property without the consent of the other spouse, the injured spouse can set aside the sale if it is done within one-year of the sale. In this case, the facts are not clear when exactly the sale took place, but it was sometime between 2013 when they separated and 2014 when Wendy initiated divorce proceedings; therefore one year has not passed. Hank may be able to set aside the sale once the court makes the determination that the office building was in fact CP. On the other hand, since Bob did not know that Wendy was married and he bought the building for consideration, he is considered a bona fide purchaser. The court may not want to injure Bob by voiding the sale, so the court may instead award Hank the value of one-half of the building.

Spouse's Obligations to Each Other

As discussed above, spouses have equal management and control of the CP assets. In addition, spouses are in a reciprocal fiduciary relationship with each other, and therefore owe each other a duty to act fairly and honestly with each other. If the court finds that Wendy acted fraudulently when she took title in her name alone and when she sold the property to Bob without Hank's knowledge, then the court could penalize her for this fraudulent behavior for breaching her fiduciary duty to Hank. Since the fiduciary duty continues until the assets have been fully divided in dissolution proceedings, Wendy still owed Hank this duty as of the date that she sold the property. However, absent a showing of fraud, the court will divide all of the assets as discussed in detail above.

QUESTION 2: SELECTED ANSWER B

California is a community property state and all property acquired during a marriage and before permanent separation is presumed to be community property ("CP"). Any property acquired by either spouse before marriage or after permanent separation is presumed to be separate property ("SP"), as is any property acquired by either spouse by gift, devise or bequest. At divorce, a court generally will award each spouse one-half of the CP in kind.

1. What are Wendy's rights, if any, as to the antique mirror?

The issue to be considered in determining Wendy's rights, if any, in the antique mirror, is whether the antique mirror is CP and whether Hank had a right to give the mirror to his friend.

The mirror is CP. Any property acquired during Hank and Wendy's marriage with CP is presumed CP. Earnings of either spouse are considered CP. Because the mirror was purchased with Hank and Wendy's earnings, it will be CP.

Under California law, both spouses have equal rights to manage and control CP. Thus, one spouse may not dispose of a piece of CP without the permission of the other spouse. Because Hank did not seek Wendy's permission in making a gift of the mirror, the gift is invalid and Wendy may try to rescind the gift and reclaim the mirror as CP. In the alternative, if the mirror is not recoverable, Hank may be required by the court to reimburse the community for the value of the mirror. Thus, in any event, unless Wendy consented to the gift, Wendy will retain her one-half interest in the antique mirror.

2. What are Hank's and Wendy's rights, if any, as to the following:

a) The house?

To determine Hank's and Wendy's rights, if any, in the house, we must determine whether the house is CP and whether any subsequent action altered that characterization.

The house was deeded to Hank and Wendy after their marriage as joint tenants. Under California law, any property held by husband and wife as joint tenants is presumed to be CP as holding in joint tenancy is antithetical to SP status; however, if the property is purchased or improved with SP, the SP is entitled to reimbursement from the community on divorce. (In contrast, on death, Lucas holds that any contribution by SP to property held in joint tenancy is a gift and there is no right to reimbursement.) The fact that Wendy's mother deeded the house to Hank and Wendy will not overcome the presumption that property held in joint tenancy will be considered to be CP. Although property given as a gift to one spouse (as one might have assumed Wendy's mother would have done) will be presumed to be SP, here Wendy's mother explicitly deeded them the house as joint tenants. Hence, it will be presumed to be CP as discussed above. Thus, prior to separation, each of Hank and Wendy had a one-half in kind interest in the house.

After the separation (which I presume for purposes of this question is a permanent separation as there are no facts to the contrary indicated in the question), Hank told Wendy that the house was henceforth her separate property and she said "O.K." In order to effectively transmute property that is CP to SP, and vice versa, under California law a valid transmutation agreement is required. Prior to 1985, an oral agreement could be effective to transmute property. However, after 1985, a transmutation must be in writing to be valid. As the purported agreement to cause the house to be SP occurred in 2013, it will be invalid. Thus, the house will remain CP and each of Hank and Wendy have a one-half in kind interest in it.

b) The accounting practice?

To determine Hank's and Wendy's rights, if any, in the accounting practice, we must determine whether the accounting practice is CP and whether any subsequent action altered that characterization.

Wendy established her accounting practice during the marriage with her labor. Any property acquired during Hank and Wendy's marriage with CP is presumed CP. Labor and earnings of either spouse are considered CP, and any goodwill created during the marriage and before permanent separation is CP. Although California allows the value of a business to be divided between SP and CP where the business was originally SP and appreciated during marriage, those rules (e.g., Pereira and Van Camp) will not apply here as the practice was established during the marriage. Thus, the value of the accounting practice that accrued until permanent separation is CP, and each of Hank and Wendy will be entitled to a one-half in kind interest therein.

However, here the facts state that Wendy's income from the accounting practice tripled after the separation. All property acquired after permanent separation is SP, including labor and wages of each spouse. Thus, Wendy's increased income post-separation and the post-separation increase in value to the accounting practice (because attributable to Wendy's labor) will be Wendy's SP and Hank will not have any interest therein.

c) The office building?

To determine Hank's and Wendy's rights, if any, in the office building, we must determine whether the office building is CP and whether any subsequent action altered that characterization.

The office building was purchased by Wendy in 2012 with funds from her earnings during marriage and she took title in her name. Under California law, all property acquired during marriage is presumed to be CP even if titled in one spouse's name. Here, we know that Wendy purchased the office building with her earnings during the marriage. Under California law, such earnings are CP. Thus, because the office building was purchased with CP it will be CP notwithstanding that title is in Wendy's name alone, the presumption that the office building is CP will not be overcome, and as of separation each of Hank and Wendy have a one-half in kind interest in it.

After separation, there are two issues to consider to establish Hank and Wendy's respective rights with respect to the office building.

After permanent separation, Wendy's earnings become SP. The issue is whether Wendy's. Under California law, when CP is improved with SP, the property remains CP but the SP is entitled to a right of reimbursement from the community. Here, after separation when Wendy remodeled the office building with her increased earnings, she was entitled to reimbursement from the community for any increased value to the office building that resulted.

Wendy subsequently sold the office building to Bob, who did not know she was married. The issue is whether that sale is valid or whether it can be rescinded. Under California law, both spouses have equal rights to manage and control CP. Thus, one spouse may not dispose of a piece of CP without the permission of the other spouse. Where, as here, one spouse sells CP without the consent of the other, the sale may generally be rescinded within the first year, unless the sale is made to a bona fide purchaser. A bona fide purchaser ("BFP") is a purchaser for value who takes without notice of the claims of any other person. In the context of community property, to be a BFP a purchaser must not know that a seller is married. Here, we know that Bob did not know Wendy was married and the deed was in her name alone. Thus, he did not have notice of Hank's interest in the property and will be a BFP. Because Bob is a BFP, the sale cannot be rescinded. Even so, Wendy will be required to reimburse the community for the purchase price (although, as noted before, she will herself be reimbursed for the value of her SP improvements).

Thus, although neither Hank or Wendy will have an interest in the office building itself, Hank will have a one-half interest in the purchase price of the office building (less the value of the remodeling, if any) and Wendy will have a one-half interest in the purchase price of the office building and a right to be reimbursed for the costs of the remodeling.

Question 3

Paul, a resident of State A, had worked as a manager at the only hotel in State A owned and operated by Hotel, Inc. (Hotel), a large national chain. Paul's compensation was $100,000 per year. Hotel was incorporated in State B, where the majority of its hotels are located. Hotel's main corporate offices are located in State C.

Hotel terminated Paul's five-year employment contract when it had two years remaining. Paul immediately found new employment with compensation of $90,000 per year.

Paul timely sued Hotel in state court in State B, alleging wrongful termination of his employment contract. In his complaint, he sought reinstatement or, in the alternative, damages of $200,000 for the two years remaining on his employment contract at the time of termination. In State B, the measure of damages for wrongful termination of an employment contract is the amount a plaintiff would have earned absent the termination, less what the plaintiff actually earned during the post-termination contract period.

After the complaint was served on Hotel at its main corporate offices in State C, Hotel timely removed the case to federal district court in State B. Paul then filed a motion in federal district court to remand to state court. The federal district court denied the motion. Paul appealed the denial to the federal court of appeals.

Paul meanwhile filed a motion in the federal district court for an injunction requiring Hotel to reinstate him to his job. The federal district court granted Paul's motion and issued the injunction. A month and a half later, Hotel appealed the injunction to the federal court of appeals.

1. Did the federal district court correctly deny Paul's motion to remand the case to state court? Discuss.

2. How should the federal court of appeals rule on Paul's appeal? Discuss.

3. How should the federal court of appeals rule on Hotel's appeal? Discuss.

QUESTION 3: SELECTED ANSWER A

1.   Did the Federal Court properly deny Paul's Motion to Remand?

The answer to this question is no. The remand should have been granted.

(a)   Diversity Jurisdiction

The issue is the nature of the federal court's jurisdiction in this case. Article III of the Constitution limits the jurisdiction of the federal courts to specific types of jurisdiction, that is, jurisdiction based on diversity of citizenship and jurisdiction based upon questions of Federal law. There are no Federal laws raised in this fact pattern, so the basis for jurisdiction must be diversity of citizenship. The other areas of justiciability will not be discussed here as they appear to be satisfied (i.e. Paul has standing to bring a claim that ripe for resolution, satisfying standing, mootness, ripeness, and a case or controversy, because he was terminated, harmed and the harm is complete).

To establish diversity jurisdiction, every plaintiff must be diverse from every defendant, based upon a party's domicile if it is an individual person, or a corporation's state of incorporation and/or principal place of business, if it is a corporation. An individual may only have one domicile; a corporation may have up to two: its state of incorporation and where it conducts its principal place of business.

Here, Paul is a resident of State A. Hotel, Inc. is incorporated in State B, so Hotel is a resident of State B. Hotel's "main corporate offices" are located in State C. If we assume that "main corporate offices" is equivalent to the corporation's "nerve center" or locus of operations, then Hotel is also a resident of State C.

Hence, it is a citizen of State A v. a citizen of State B and State C, even though there is only one defendant.

The Federal diversity statute (28 USC 1332) not only has a citizenship test; it also has an amount in controversy test. This means that the amount in controversy for a cause of action (or aggregated causes of action) must be greater than $75,000, exclusive of interest and costs. If a plaintiff alleges such an amount, the court will generally not look behind that amount, unless it amounts to a legal certainty that plaintiff cannot recover it.

Here, Paul has asserted a claim for damages as a result of the breach of employment contract for $200,000 for the two years remaining on his employment contract or, in the alternative, he seeks reinstatement, which means he wants his old job back.

We are told that the law in State B is that the measure of damages for wrongful termination of an employment contract is the amount a plaintiff would have earned absent the termination, less what the plaintiff actually earned. Here, Paul has mitigated as he was contractually required to do and found new employment for $90,000 per year. But this will not defeat the amount in controversy for several reasons. First, Paul seeks as one of his remedies reinstatement to a job valued at $100,000 per year for two years — thus readily satisfying the "value of his complaint" in excess of $75,000. In addition, we do not know to a "legal certainty" that Paul will actually be employed by the new employer at $90,000 per year for the next two years. He might be fired again or he may not like the job and quit — perhaps it isn't a truly comparable position. And finally, it isn't even abundantly clear that State B law will apply. Paul was working in State A and he is a resident of State A. Generally speaking, the law of the state in which an employee performs services governs employment contract disputes (unless provided otherwise in the employment agreement). Accordingly, the amount in controversy is satisfied.

(b)   Removal

A party is permitted to remove an action to federal court from state court pursuant to 28 USC 1441 if federal jurisdiction exists and the party acts to effectuate removal within thirty days after receiving notice (not service) of a state court action upon which removal may be based. A removal is effective upon the filing of the notice of removal in state court. The action will then proceed as an originally filed federal action thereafter, except certain pleading timing rules are modified. But there is one other requirement not met here: only nonresident defendants may remove.

Hotel is a resident of both State B (where it is incorporated) and State C (its principle place of business). The case was filed in state B state court. Because Hotel is a resident of State B, Hotel cannot remove a case from State B court to a Federal court in State B, and the court should have granted Paul's motion to remand.

2.   Paul's Appeal of the Denial of Remand

The Federal court of appeals should dismiss Paul's appeal because a denial of remand is not a final judgment from which an appeal may be taken to the Federal Circuit Court of Appeals ("CTA"). It would rather be deemed to be an interlocutory appeal. With a few limited circumstances, one of which is discussed below, a litigant may only prosecute an appeal to the CTA upon the issuance of a final judgment by the district court (i.e., final judgment after trial, a dismissal of a case pursuant to Fed R. Civ P 12b6 or a Fed. R. Civ. P. 56 summary judgment motion). Exceptions may exist, i.e., the district court may give permission to a litigant to file an appeal prior to a final judgment if it appears that it would be more efficient to proceed in that manner, i.e., the CTA may upon ruling, direct the district court to proceed in a particular manner that might impact the trial of the case. A denial of a motion to remand, however, is not an immediately appealable order and absent permission from the district court, it will not be entertained by the CTA. Paul otherwise must wait until the matter is concluded.

3.   Hotel's Appeal of the Injunction

The CTA will deny Hotel's appeal as untimely. But it otherwise would have likely sustained Hotel's appeal on substantive grounds.

A party has thirty days to appeal from a district court's judgment or appealable order to the CTA. Here, we are told that Hotel did not appeal the injunction until a month and a half after its issuance. Hotel was late. Injunctions are an exception to the final judgment rule — if a party is mandated by a federal court to do something, that party may immediately (or within thirty days) appeal that order. This order is in the nature of a mandatory injunction.

A mandatory injunction differs from a prohibitory injunction in that the federal court mandates or orders a party to act. A prohibitory injunction is an injunction based upon a directive to a party to cease doing something. In this case, the court has ordered Hotel to reinstate Paul to his position as manager at Hotel A. This effectively requires Hotel to reinstate an employee it has just fired.

Courts typically do not grant mandatory injunctions for personal services contracts, like the one at issue here. There are several reasons for this view. It is simply not feasible to enforce these orders: requiring an employer to have an employee on the premises who may or may not discharge his work obligations may impact the employer's business. This is particularly apt here where the employee is a manager at a hotel — he may well come into contact with the public and may be in a very sensitive position. Second, a mandatory injunction in this context inserts the court directly into the business of the employer — it just isn't feasible for a court to determine whether the employee is being treated well, paid right, advanced, compensated, managed properly, carrying out the Hotel's instructions, etc. Setting those policy issues aside, however, there is an adequate money damages remedy here — a written employment contract with two years remaining, and clearly sets compensation for those two years (regardless of mitigation issues or which state's law applies). And there is no irreparable harm — again, even on balance of all the interests here, this a simple breach of employment contract case, remedied easily through money damages. Balancing the harms, as the court would do on an injunction, clearly favors Hotel: it is far more burdensome to require Hotel to take back Paul and supervise him where Paul can ultimately recover a money judgment against a presumably solvent defendant, a large national hotel chain.

QUESTION 3: SELECTED ANSWER B

Denial of Motion to Remand

The federal court erred in denying Paul's motion to remand to state court.

In order for a case to be removed to federal court, the federal court to which the case is removed (the district court for the district in which the state court is located) must be a court in which the case originally could have been filed. This requires that the court have subject matter jurisdiction, personal jurisdiction over the defendant, and that venue be appropriate in that court.

Subject matter jurisdiction can be based either on diversity jurisdiction or federal question jurisdiction. Federal question jurisdiction exists when, from the face of a well-pleaded complaint, plaintiff's claim "arises under" federal law. Here, there is no basis for federal question jurisdiction. Paul's claim is one purely in contract, based on a state law cause of action for wrongful termination. There is no indication whatsoever from the facts that his claim arises under federal law or that he is enforcing any federal right. Accordingly, there is no federal question jurisdiction.

Accordingly, the federal court can have jurisdiction only if there is diversity jurisdiction. Diversity jurisdiction is present in a suit between citizens of different states where the amount in controversy is at least $75,000. First, it does appear that Paul and Hotel, Inc. are citizens of different states. An individual is a citizen of the state in which he is domiciled, i.e., where he resides and intends to remain permanently. Here, the facts indicate that Paul is a resident of State A, and there is nothing to indicate that he resides in any other state or does not intend to remain permanently in State A; thus, he is a citizen of State A for purposes of diversity jurisdiction. A corporation, by contrast, is a citizen of <u>both</u> (1) the state in which it is incorporated and (2) the state in which it has its principal place of business, i.e., its "nerve center" from which responsible managers control the corporation's affairs. Here, Hotel is incorporated in State B, and its main corporate offices are in State C. There is no indication from the facts that Hotel has its principal place of business in another state, and it thus appears that its principal place of business would be its corporate offices in State C. (It is certainly clear that Hotel does not have its principal place of business in State A, in which it has only a single hotel.) Thus, Hotel appears to be a citizen of both State B and State C for purposes of diversity jurisdiction. Therefore, Paul and Hotel are citizens of different states, and there is the requisite "complete diversity" for purposes of diversity jurisdiction.

However, it is unclear that the requisite $75,000 amount in controversy is satisfied on these facts. Paul's complaint advances claims for both damages and injunctive relief. When damages are at issue, the plaintiff's good faith assessment of damages will govern the amount-in-controversy analysis, unless it appears clear to a legal certainty that those damages are unobtainable. With respect to injunctive relief, the monetary value of the relief can be based on the greater of either (1) the benefit to the plaintiff or (2) the harm to the defendant.

Here, Paul's claim for damages does not appear to satisfy the amount-in-controversy. A plaintiff seeking damages is entitled only to his expectation damages (as well as incidental damages). Every plaintiff has a duty to mitigate damages, which Paul did here by obtaining another job at a rate of $90,000 per year. Accordingly, expectation damages — which are designed to return the plaintiff to the position he would have occupied absent the breach of contract — would be only $10,000 per year, or $20,000 total. It appears that State B has adopted this measure of damages and, under the Erie doctrine, State B's substantive law should apply to this case, since a federal case sitting in diversity is obligated to apply a state's substantive law. There is no federal law in direct conflict with State B's rule of damages; accordingly, it is necessary to consider whether applying State B's damages computation methodology would be outcome determinative, whether it would lead to forum shopping (causing plaintiffs to flock to federal court), and whether the state has a particular interest in having its law applied. It is clear based on these factors that the damages methodology is substantive in nature and should be applied — the amount of damages that a plaintiff can recover in a matter are certainly outcome determinative, are highly likely to affect a plaintiff's choice of forum, and reflect the state's policy determination as to the matter at issue. In any event, the value of Paul's monetary damages claim is the same — and short of the amount in controversy requirement — whether one applies general contract law principles or State B's damages rule.

However, the injunctive relief Paul seeks does satisfy the amount-in-controversy requirement. If the injunction were granted, the benefit to Paul would only be the additional $20,000 in income over the next two years; but if granted, the harm to Hotel would be in the amount of $200,000, i.e., the two years of additional salary that it would be required to pay to Paul. Accordingly, the $75,000 amount in controversy is satisfied.

Nevertheless, although both requirements for diversity jurisdiction are met here, the federal district court erred in denying Paul's motion to remand. A defendant (or defendants) may not remove a case from state court to federal court if any defendant is a citizen of the forum state. Here, as discussed above, Hotel is a citizen of State B. Thus, Hotel was not entitled to remove the case, removal was procedurally improper, and the district court should have granted Paul's motion to remand.

Paul's Appeal

The Court of Appeals should refuse to hear Paul's appeal.

As an initial matter, a grant of a motion to remand is never appealable. Here, by contrast, the district court denied Paul's motion. However, under the final judgment rule, one has a right to appeal as of right only from a final judgment of the district court. A final judgment is one that is final as to all claims at issue and all parties involved, i.e., one that leaves nothing more for the trial court to do. A denial of a motion to remand is not such a final judgment, and is thus not appealable as of right.

Moreover, there is no indication in the facts that any of the exceptions to the final judgment rule apply here. For example, the Court of Appeals may choose to hear an appeal based on the "collateral order doctrine" where a decision of the district court is collateral to the merits of the case, involves an important issue of law that has been finally decided, and the party appealing would be effectively precluded from achieving review of the decision absent an immediate appeal. Here, however, while the district court's denial of Paul's motion to remand is collateral to the merits of the case and final, Paul will have the opportunity to obtain appellate review of that decision through a normal appeal at the conclusion of the matter. Accordingly, the collateral order doctrine does not apply. Nor is there any indication from the facts that the district court has certified this ruling for immediate appeal under the Interlocutory Appeals Act (or that the Court of Appeals has accepted such an appeal), or that any statutory exception to the final judgment rule applies.

Hotel's Appeal

The Court of Appeals should dismiss Hotel's appeal, because it is untimely.

As an initial matter, the order granting Paul's requested injunction is an appealable order. Although the grant of this motion would otherwise not be a final judgment under the final judgment rule, there is an exception for orders granting, modifying, or dissolving injunctions. Accordingly, though the case remains pending, the district court's order granting Paul's motion for an injunction was an appealable order.

However, Hotel, Inc. did not timely appeal from the district court's order granting Paul's injunction. A party must appeal within 30 days of an appealable order. Here, the facts indicate that Hotel, Inc. noticed its appeal "[a] month and a half later." The facts do not contain any indication of excusable neglect on Hotel's part, and Hotel's appeal should thus be dismissed as untimely.

Question 4

Jane owned a machine shop. It had one slightly buckled wall. It had been built years prior to Town's adoption of a zoning ordinance that permits office buildings and retail stores, but not manufacturing facilities.

Ira purchased the machine shop from Jane for $500,000. He gave her $50,000 in cash and a promissory note for an additional $50,000 secured by a deed of trust. He borrowed the other $400,000 from Acme Bank (Acme), which recorded a mortgage. Acme was aware of Jane's promissory note and deed of trust prior to the close of escrow.

Donna owns a parcel adjoining Ira's machine shop. She recently began excavation for construction of an office building. Ira complained to Donna that the excavation was causing the shop's wall to buckle further, but she did nothing in response.

Shortly thereafter, Ira's machine shop collapsed. Ira applied to Town for a building permit to rebuild the shop, but Town refused. He then defaulted on his obligations to Jane and Acme.

Ira has sued Donna seeking damages, and he has sued Town seeking issuance of a building permit. Acme has filed a foreclosure suit against Ira, and Jane has demanded a proportionate share of the proceeds from any foreclosure sale.

1. How is the court likely to rule on Ira's claim for damages against Donna? Discuss.

2. How is the court likely to rule on Ira's request that Town issue a building permit? Discuss.

3. How is the court likely to rule on Jane's claim for a proportionate share of the proceeds from any foreclosure sale? Discuss.

QUESTION 4: SELECTED ANSWER A

1. Ira's Claim for Damages against Donna

Ira owned the machine shop that adjoined Donna's parcel of land. When Donna excavated her parcel it caused Ira's machine shop to collapse. Ira has many multiple causes of action that he may pursue against Donna in attempt to recover from the collapse of his machine shop. They include a strict liability claim based on lateral support principles, or based on negligence.

Strict Liability and Lateral Support:

Landowners have a right to the support of the surface of their property. When an adjoining landowner engages in action that causes the adjoining property to subside, the owner who caused the subsidence may be strictly liable for the damage caused. In order for strict liability to apply, the injured party whose property has subsided must show that the actions of the adjoining landowner caused the subsidence, and that the subsidence would have occurred even if no structures were built on the injured party's land. If the subsidence would not have occurred but for the weight of the structure built on the land, then strict liability will not attach and the injured party will have to pursue another cause of action to recover.

Here, Donna began excavation for construction of an office building on her parcel that was adjacent to Ira's machine shop. Despite complaints from Ira, Donna continued her planned excavation. Based on Ira's statements that the excavation was causing the wall of his machine shop to "buckle further," which eventually led to the collapse of the machine shop, it seems clear that the excavation is what actually caused the structure to fall. Ira can recover for strict liability as long as the subsidence would have occurred even if the machine shop were not built on the land. This is likely where Ira's cause of action will fail. Facts stipulate that the wall of the machine shop was slightly buckled, and the excavation caused the wall to "further buckle." Facts do not indicate that the land on which Ira's shop actually subsided, only that the action caused the machine shop to collapse. It does not appear that the land would have been damaged or lost lateral support if the machine shop was not built on the land.

In conclusion, Ira cannot recover based on his right to lateral support in strict liability because the collapse of the structure and the land likely would not have occurred if the structure was not built. No facts indicate the land would have subsided despite the shop. Ira must look to another cause of action.

Negligence:

Ira may attempt to assert a negligence claim against Donna. Negligence occurs when a party breaches a duty owed to another and the breach is the actual and proximate cause of damages suffered by another party.

Duty:

Donna has a duty to act as a reasonably prudent landowner who adjoins other parcels with structure on them. Ira is an owner of an adjoining parcel, she had a duty to act as a reasonably prudent landowner to the adjacent owners.

Foreseeable plaintiff:

Under the majority view of Cardozo, a party only owes a duty to foreseeable plaintiffs. Foreseeable plaintiffs are those that reside within the zone of danger of the defendant's actions. Here, Ira was the adjacent landowner to Donna. When Donna began excavation all adjacent landowners were foreseeable plaintiffs because it is foreseeable that construction could cause injury to the adjacent land or landowners. Ira was a foreseeable plaintiff.

Breach:

Donna possibly breached her duty to act as a reasonably prudent landowner when she continued excavation despite the fact that she was informed it was causing a wall of Ira's to buckle and was likely going to cause damage. Facts do not indicate whether or not the excavation was executed with reasonable care or not, but the fact that Donna continued after being informed that her actions were causing damage may mean that she breached her duty of care to Ira.

Actual Cause:

Actual cause is also termed the "but for" cause. The issue is whether but for Donna's actions the building would have collapsed. Ira informed Donna that the construction was causing the wall to buckle further, and the continued excavation led to the collapse of the building. Donna's actions were the but for cause of the collapse.

Proximate Cause:

Proximate cause is called the legal cause and the issue is foreseeability. Here, it is foreseeable that a person doing excavation may end up causing damage to the structures of adjoining parcels. Ira will argue that Donna's actions were completely foreseeable. Donna on the other hand will argue that the proximate cause was not her excavation, but rather the fact that the machine shop already had a "slightly buckled wall." Donna will argue that it is not foreseeable that adjacent landowners have improperly supported structures that will collapse during excavation of adjoining parcels. Donna's argument that the buckled wall makes the collapse unforeseeable probably will not work, but it may be effective as a defense (discussed below.) Moreover, Donna knew that her actions were causing the wall to buckle more after Ira told her, so ultimately her actions were foreseeable because she was informed of them.

Damages: Damages must be causal, foreseeable, certain, and unavoidable.

Here, Donna's actions caused the entire shop to collapse, and it is very possible that a court will find that she breached her duty to Ira and that her actions were the actual and proximate cause of Ira's damages. Absent any defenses, Donna will be required to pay Ira for either the cost of repair of the building (which is substantial), or the reduced value of Ira's property now that the shop has collapsed.

Defenses: Comparative Negligence

Donna has a good argument that Ira was himself negligent and she should be absolved of liability or that her liability should be substantially reduced. Ira knew that the machine shop had a slightly buckled wall that would likely reduce its structural soundness. Ira had a duty to investigate the structural integrity of the building, and insure that it was not at risk for collapsing easily. This is a very strong argument and Donna will likely have her damages reduced by the amount of Ira's negligence, which is significant.

In conclusion, Ira may recover from Donna under a negligence theory but Donna's damages will be offset by the amount of Ira's own negligence.

2. Ira's Request to have Town Issue a Building Permit.

Here, Ira's machine shop has been destroyed, and he wishes to rebuild it. Because of the current zoning ordinance, Ira's machine shop is not permitted in the area where he wants to build it. The issue is whether Ira should be granted a permit to operate the machine shop.

Zoning Ordinances:

Zoning ordinances are an effective way for states and localities to regulate the land use of their jurisdiction. However, a person who seeks to violate a zoning ordinance may seek a variance that will be granted or denied in the form of a permit.

Variance:

A variance is an individual exception to a zoning ordinance. There are two types, area variances and use variances. Area variances are more likely to be granted because it is simply an exception given to allow a building to exist in dimensions that slightly violate the zoning ordinance. Use ordinances are less likely to be granted — a use variance is a permit allowing a person to operate a structure for a purpose that is not permitted by the zoning ordinance. Here, Ira wishes to get a permit to allow him to use his property for manufacturing, which is a use that is not permitted. In order to get a use permit, Ira must show that he will (1) suffer a hardship without the ordinance, (2) that the variance would not damage or harm the neighborhood, and (3) that he is not at fault or a bad actor in his request.

(1) Suffer a hardship

Here, Ira has paid a substantial amount of money in order to purchase the machine shop and operate it at the location where it currently resides. But for the fact that the machine shop collapsed, Ira would still be able to operate it most likely as a nonconforming use (discussed below). Preventing Ira from being able to rebuild and operate the shop as he had previously would cause him significant injury and he will surely suffer an economic hardship if not allowed to resume his business.

(2) Won't Harm the Neighborhood

Here, the neighborhood permits office buildings and retail stores, just not manufacturing. If the neighborhood were zoned only for residential use by families, it is likely that granting such a variance would cause harm to the neighborhood because families would have to deal with the constant manufacturing noise. But, because the area allows offices and retail stores, it is unlikely that the manufacturing would likely cause significant harm to the neighborhood, unless the manufacturing involved toxic materials or chemicals. This factor weighs in favor of Ira.

(3) Ira is not at Fault

Here, Ira was operating the machine shop until Donna's excavation caused the shop to collapse. Ira did not buy the property knowing about the ordinance and now seeks a variance to benefit knowing all along such action would be in violation. And, but for the collapse of the structure, Ira likely would have been able to continue to run the business as a nonconforming use. Ira is not at fault in seeking the variance.

Conclusion:

In conclusion, the court should rule that the Town should issue a building permit because all of the elements required for a proper use variance are satisfied, and Ira is not a bad actor.

Nonconforming Use:

The other argument that Ira may present is that his operation of the machine shop is a nonconforming use because it was in existence prior to the change of the ordinance. Nonconforming uses that are in effect prior to an ordinance change are allowed to continue unless they cause harm to residents or adjoining property. Even then, an amortization period is generally allowed to allow the owner to find a new location for the activity. Here, Ira was properly operating the manufacturing business prior to the ordinance, and the fact that the building collapsed should not deprive him of being able to rebuild a similar structure and continue with the nonconforming operation he had prior to the collapse. There is no evidence the manufacturing is causing harm to other residents.

In conclusion, the court also should have the Town issue a building permit because Ira's prior nonconforming use should still be considered in effect.

3. Jane's Claim for Proportionate Share of the Proceeds from Foreclosure.

Deed of Trust and Mortgage:

When Ira purchased the property from Jane, he gave her a 50K promissory note secured by a deed of trust. He borrowed the other 400K from Acme which recorded a mortgage. Mortgages and Deeds of Trust operate similarly.

A <u>Deed of Trust</u> is an arrangement where a third party holds a deed in a trust to stand as collateral for a debt owed. With a deed a trust, if the debtor (Ira) fails to make payments and ends up in default on the loan, the party that made the loan, Jane, can initiate foreclosure and execute a <u>private</u> sale of the property.

A <u>Mortgage</u> is an arrangement where a party who has or is buying property gets a loan and has the property itself stand as security for the debt. If a debtor fails to make the loan payments and ends up in default, then the holder of the mortgage, the mortgagee, may initiate <u>public</u> foreclosure proceedings against the property.

Here, Ira failed to make payments on the loan and was thus in default. Acme was within its right to initiate foreclosing proceedings against the property to recover for the debt owed. The order of payment from a foreclosure sale is determined by a number of factors, including whether the loan was a purchase money security interest.

<u>Priority</u>:

Upon a foreclosure sale, how proceeds from the sale are distributed is determined by the priority of the creditor's interest. Priority is determined by (1) whether or not the loan was a purchase money security interest and (2) when the interest or mortgage was recorded. All purchase money security interests have priority over other creditor interests executed at the same time.

Here, Jane executed a valid deed of trust, and Acme executed a valid mortgage. The mortgage was recorded and had notice of the deed of trust secured by Jane. Because both loans were provided in order for Ira to obtain the purchase of the property, both interests should be considered purchase money security interests. If Acme had recorded the mortgage on the property without notice of the deed of trust secured by Jane, Acme would have had priority over all other creditors. However, because Acme had notice of the deed of trust, and because both loans will be considered purchase money security interests, Jane's Deed of Trust will have priority.

Order of Payment:

Foreclosure proceeds are not distributed in proportion. So, the court will not rule that a proportionate share of the foreclosure proceeds should be given to her. However, that does not mean that Jane's interest will necessarily be adversely affected. When a creditor forecloses on a property and provides notice to any junior interest, at the sale of the property the junior interest is extinguished. Here, Acme initiated the public foreclosure sale, and had Jane's deed of trust been a junior interest, then Jane was required to notice, but her interest would be extinguished at the end of the sale, whether or not she received proceeds. A senior interest remains intact on the property when a junior interest initiates the foreclosure. When a foreclosure is executed, the priority of payment is that (1) all fees are paid for the foreclosure, (2) Senior creditor interests are paid first and in order to the junior interests, and (3) anything left over is given the debtor, or owner of the property.

Here, Jane's interest in the property has priority to Acme's because her deed of trust was executed first, Acme was aware of the deed of trust, and both interests are purchase money security interest. Accordingly, Jane's interest will not be extinguished by the foreclosure sale by Acme. If the proceeds from the sale produce enough to pay both the debts of Acme and Jane, then both will be paid, and any remainder will be given to Ira. If not, Acme's foreclosure sale will be subject to Jane's deed of trust, and the sale will not extinguish that interest. Jane will be able to foreclose on the property regardless of who purchases the shop during the public foreclosure sale.

CONCLUSION:

In conclusion, though the court will not order Acme to split the proceeds from the foreclosure sale with Jane proportionally, Jane's deed of trust is superior to Acme's mortgage, and the public foreclosure would not extinguish her interest in the machine shop.

QUESTION 4: SELECTED ANSWER B

1. Ira v. Donna

The first issue is establishing what obligations, if any, Donna owes to Ira as a neighboring property owner.

Ira is claiming damages against Donna for the damage caused by Donna's excavation for the construction of an office building. Duties between neighboring property owners can arise in several ways, namely, through contract or tort law. Under contract law, if parties enter into covenants with each other to do something or refrain from doing something on their land, they may be obligated under contract law to fulfill those obligations. Another way in which neighboring property owners may owe each other a duty is through tort law. If Donna and Jane (Ira's predecessor) or Donna and Ira had created a covenant not to interfere with one another's sublateral support, Ira may have a claim for damages under that theory. However, it does not appear that they have an explicit agreement.

Tort law will also impose duties on neighboring property owners in some instances. For example, if one property owner's use of the property is in a way that causes a nuisance, that may give rise to liability under tort law. Likewise, neighbors have a general obligation to refrain from engaging in hazardous or inherently dangerous activities on their property that may interfere with others outside of their property. Additionally, property owners may have a duty under either a strict liability or negligence theory for interfering with a property owner's sublateral support.

Inherently Dangerous Activities

Ira may argue that Donna's use of the neighboring property (using an excavator) constitutes an inherently dangerous activity. When a property owner engages in an inherently dangerous activity she will be held strictly liable for injuries resulting as a consequence of that activity's inherently dangerous propensities. In order to be considered inherently dangerous, an activity must be: 1) unusual for the community; 2) one that cannot be made safer by safety measures; 3) one whose utility is outweighed by the danger it is likely to cause.

In this case, Donna is excavating her property to build an office building. Donna is doing so in a zone that specifically permits office buildings. One may assume that if office buildings are allowed in the zone, their construction is also a usual activity for that area. Further, there is utility in developing a community for business and thus, there is utility in building office buildings. Further, the construction of office buildings can be made safer by taking safety precautions, by having licensed contractors, putting up warning signs, etc. Therefore, using an excavator will likely not constitute an inherently dangerous activity and Ira does not have a cause of action under this theory.

Interference with Sublateral Supports

An alternative theory will arise by asserting that Donna has interfered with Ira's subadjacent property rights. In cases where a neighbor excavates and causes a disturbance in their neighbor's sublateral support for their property, the neighbor whose property was damaged may have a cause of action under either a negligence theory or a strict liability theory. Which theory applies depends on whether or not the neighbor (Ira) can show by clear and convincing evidence that her property and the weight of his buildings did not contribute to the damage. That is, there would have been damage regardless of whether or not the buildings were constructed. If the plaintiff (Ira) cannot show that his buildings did not contribute to the ultimate injury, then he must make out a case in negligence. If he can, then he may make out a case in strict liability.

In this case, when Jane owned the machine shop it already had a slightly buckled wall. Therefore, when Ira took the building, the wall was likely still buckled or even made worse with the passing of time. Because of this, the unsecured nature of the construction likely contributed in some way to the building's ultimate destruction.

Therefore, strict liability is not available to Ira because he cannot demonstrate that the buildings on his property in no way contributed to the damage.

Therefore, Ira must make out a case in negligence. In order to make out a case in negligence, a plaintiff must show that: 1) defendant had a duty to the plaintiff; 2) defendant breached that duty; 3) the breach was the actual and proximate cause of the damage; 4) there were damages.

In this case, a duty has already been established under the sublateral support doctrine. The standard of care is an objective, reasonable person standard. Negligence causes of action incentivize individuals to act in a reasonable way in their interactions with others. The standard of care in this case would be what a reasonable person excavating property next to a neighbor's property would do.

The next issue is whether or not the defendant breached that duty. In this case, it appears as though Donna initially was acting as a reasonable person; as discussed, she was excavating property to build an office building in an area zoned for that use. However, Ira complained to Donna that the excavation was causing the shop's wall to buckle further. After Donna was put on notice of creating this damage, the question becomes whether a reasonable person would have done something to attempt to avoid the damage. In this case, Donna did nothing at all. It seems that a reasonable person would have assessed whether it was possible to move the location of the excavation or adjust construction in some other way to avoid the damage. Because there is no evidence that Donna did this, a court may find that she breached her duty toward Ira.

The next issue is whether her breach was the actual cause and proximate cause of the damage. Actual cause is but-for cause: but for the breach, would the damage have occurred? Actual cause may also be substantial cause if there are two or more contributing causes, either one of which may have been sufficient to cause the damage. In this case, it appears as though Donna's actions were the but for cause of the building's collapse. Ira complained to Donna that the excavation was causing the building to further buckle. While it may ultimately be an issue of fact regarding whether it was the buckling of the wall or the excavation, for the purposes of getting the question to a jury a court would likely assume this element was met.

The next question is whether the excavation was the proximate cause of the injury. Proximate cause is the philosophical nexus between the act taken and the damage done -- it requires more than just actual cause and requires that the cause be something foreseeable from the defendant's actions such that it comports with notions of common sense and justice to hold the defendant liable for his actions. Under Palsgraf, the relevant question is whether the injury was foreseeable to the actor. A minority view would hold any damage is foreseeable if it resulted from the action. In this case, because Donna had notice of the damage the excavation was causing, and the excavation was occurring right under the building, it seems foreseeable the damage to the building was likely. Therefore, the proximate cause element is likely met.

Finally, Ira must show there was damage resulting from the breach. In this case, there was actual destruction of his building, resulting in substantial damage, so this element is also met.

Note, most jurisdictions would reduce the amount of damages that Ira receives based on a pure comparative negligence standard, which reduces the amount of recovery that plaintiff receives by her amount of fault. In a traditional comparative negligence state, the recovery would be reduced entirely if the plaintiff was at all at fault. In this case, it does seem as though Ira was partially to blame for not strengthening his wall or doing anything to avoid the damage. Therefore, his damage award will likely be reduced based on the findings of a jury.

2. Ira v. Town

Is the ordinance valid under the Constitution?

Ira's case against the town arises from the Town's refusal to permit him to rebuild a machine shop in a zone that permits office buildings and retail stores, but not manufacturing facilities.

The first issue is whether or not the town's adoption of a zoning ordinance is permissible under the Constitution. The Constitution permits state actors to take or incur on a private citizen's property rights for the public good provided they are given just compensation, measured by the value to the property owner, not the benefit conferred to the government. Generally, zoning ordinances, although they are not complete takings under the Constitution, are analyzed under this framed work.

The general rule is that if the government possesses a private actor's property, no matter in what degree, it will constitute a taking under the Constitution and the property owner will be entitled to compensation. In this case, because the Town has not physically possessed Ira's property, this does not constitute a complete taking.

However, a regulatory regime that destroys all economic viability will also constitute a complete taking under the Constitution and will require the property owner be justly compensated. In this case, the zoning ordinance is a regulation. However, it does not completely destroy the value of Ira's property because he could still build an office building, retail store, sell the property, etc. Therefore, it is not a complete taking under this theory either.

Finally, a partial taking may also require compensation under the Penn Central balancing test if a property owner's property interests are interfered with and his property value decreased. Courts look at: 1) the investment-backed expectations of the property owner; 2) the nature of the government action; 3) the benefit to the public and harm to the individual property owner and what the owner should rightfully have to bear for the benefit of the public. In this case, it is unclear whether Ira's property rights decreased. Clearly, he cannot do what he wants with the property, but that does not mean it does not have other values. Therefore, a court would likely find the Town's refusal to issue a building permit proper under the Constitution.

Is a variance warranted?

The question becomes then, whether or not Ira is entitled to continue using the facility pursuant to a zoning variance for prior use. A zoning variance may be granted if the owner of property can show that the use of their property in the manner previously used will cause undue hardship to the owner and would not cause significant harm to the community if the variance was granted. Notably, when the zoning ordinance is valid, as this one is (see previous discussion), a Town has some discretion in balancing the harms to the application and to the community.

In this case, the zoning ordinance permits office buildings and retail stores, but not manufacturing facilities. The reasoning behind this ordinance seems apparent: manufacturing facilities are generally larger, more disruptive, more likely to emit noise, debris, etc. A town has a reasonable basis for preferring to have a community comprised of stores and office buildings, were people can shop and work without distraction and interference. Therefore, the harm to the community if the variance were granted seems great.

However, Ira does have an argument that because of the pre-existing use of the machine shop by Jane, he is entitled to a variance under the theory that he was grandfathered into the ordinance. However, there are three problems with this argument. First, as previously discussed, the Town has good reason for not wanting manufacturing facilities in the retail/office area of town and variances are discretionary. Second, there are privity issues between Jane and Ira and the Town. It was Jane, not Ira that had been using the building as a machine shop (presumably a manufacturing facility, though Ira might raise a classification argument), when the ordinance was passed. Third, the pre-existing use generally must be consistent if a variance is granted for pre-existing use. When the machine shop collapsed, it was no longer used as a manufacturing facility and Ira likely lost his ability to claim any sort of entitlement to use the property as a manufacturing facility under the pre-existing use doctrine.

In conclusion, a court will likely deny Ira's request that the Town issue a building permit.

3. Jane v. Bank (re: proportionate share of the foreclosure proceeds)

The issue this question raises is how to be characterize the security interests that Jane and Acme have in the machine shop property and what the priority of those interests are.

Generally, mortgages are security interests in property, used by a mortgagee to secure a debt that she has issued to a mortgagor. In this case, Ira purchased the machine shop from Jane for $500,000, but as he clearly did not have that much money, he took out loans. A loan may be either secured or unsecured. An unsecured loan is one that does not have any collateral that a lender may use as compensation in the event of default. A secured loan is one that has property of some sort as collateral for the repayment of a loan. Unsecured loans take a second seat to secured loans when property is foreclosed upon.

Generally, mortgages are prioritized in the order they were made. A bank that loans money to a home purchaser will take a first mortgage on that home. If the purchaser later borrows more money, that lender may also secure the repayment with a mortgage on the home, but it will be subject to the first lender. Once the first lender is paid in full, the second lender will be entitled to proceeds. This is why second mortgages often have higher interest rates or are otherwise on less favorable terms -- they are less secure because they are subordinate to another's interests in the property. The proceeds come from a foreclosure sale, which occurs when the property securing the debt is sold to pay off the lenders.

Finally, there are special types of loans/mortgages called "purchase money mortgages". The mortgages occur when the money lent to a mortgagee is used for the purchase of the item itself. This typically occurs with owner financing -- if a homeowner sells her home and loans money to the purchaser to buy it, there is a purchase money mortgage in the house. These types of mortgages will take priority, even if there is a primary lender that attached prior to the purchase money mortgage being issued.

In this case, Ira purchased the machine shop from Jane for $500,000. Obviously Ira did not have that cash up front. Instead, he paid $50,000 in cash to Jane, which is hers to keep and is not up for grabs at the foreclosure sale. Next, he gave her a promissory note for an additional $50,000 secured by a deed of trust. Then he borrowed another $400,000 from Acme Bank, which recorded a mortgage.

If the $50,000 from Jane was secured by an interest in the machine shop, the very property the loan was made to purchase, this loan will take priority and Jane will be entitled to the first $50,000 received in the foreclosure sale.

Acme will argue that it is the primary lender and that it is entitled to all the money from the foreclosure sale, until it exceeds its $400,000 loan, at which case it may spill over to secondary lenders. There are two problems with this argument: 1) First, as discussed above, Jane's loan to Ira was a purchase money mortgage and takes priority over the Bank's loan. Even if it were not a purchase money mortgage, Jane was still the first lender. 2) Second, Acme knew of Jane's promissory note and deed of trust prior to the close of escrow. Notably, although Jane did not appear to record her mortgage, a recording is not required to secure an interest. Rather, a recording system serves to give subsequent mortgagees and purchasers notice, something Acme already had.

The issue then becomes, what is the effect of Acme's knowledge on its mortgage in the property? Generally, in order to take priority, a mortgagee must be a holder in due course, or a bona fide mortgagee, who takes without knowledge of any other interests in the property. In this case, because Acme knew about Jane's deed of trust, Acme was not a bona fide mortgagee or holder in due course; therefore, Acme's mortgage could be subordinated on this ground.

Note: Generally the holder in due course requirements are intended to protect a subsequent mortgagee who takes from a first mortgagee. A holder in due course will be protected if he takes a negotiable instrument, made out to the holder, without notice of impediments, for valuable consideration and in good faith. A holder in due course will be free from personal defenses raised by the mortgagor (e.g., lack of consideration, waiver), but will take subject to non-personal defenses (e.g., duress). In this case, Acme did not take the mortgage from another mortgagee, but rather was the first mortgagee. Therefore, this doctrine does not apply, but its principles still do. Generally, courts do not reward mortgagees or other property holders who take knowing of another's interest in land.

In sum, Acme, although it was the first to record, under either a notice or race-notice jurisdiction, Acme is not entitled to bona fide purchaser/mortgagee status because it took knowing of Jane's mortgage. Further, Jane is protected by her status as a purchase money mortgagee. Therefore, a court will likely rule that she is entitled to $50,000 from a foreclosure sale.

Question 5

For many years, the Old Ways Fellowship, a neopagan religious organization, received permission from the City's Building Authority to display a five-foot diameter symbol of the sun in the lobby of City's Municipal Government Building during the week surrounding the Winter Solstice. The display was accompanied by a sign stating "Old Ways Fellowship wishes you a happy Winter Solstice."

Last year the Building Authority adopted a new "Policy on Seasonal Displays," which states:

> Religious displays and symbols are not permitted in any government building. Such displays and symbols impermissibly convey the appearance of government endorsement of religion.

Previously, the Building Authority had allowed access to a wide variety of public and private speakers and displays in the lobby of the Municipal Government Building. Based on the new policy, however, it denied the Old Ways Fellowship a permit for the sun display.

After it was informed by counsel that courts treat Christmas trees as secular symbols, rather than religious symbols, the Building Authority decided to erect a Christmas tree in the lobby of the Municipal Government Building, while continuing to prohibit the Old Ways Fellowship sun display.

The Old Ways Fellowship contests the Building Authority's policy and its decision regarding the Christmas tree. It has offered to put up a disclaimer sign explaining that the Winter Solstice greeting is not endorsed by City. The Building Authority has turned down this offer.

The Old Ways Fellowship has filed suit claiming violation of the First Amendment to the United States Constitution.

What arguments may the Old Ways Fellowship reasonably raise in support of its claim and how are they likely to fare? Discuss.

QUESTION 5: SELECTED ANSWER A

OLD WAYS FELLOWSHIP'S FIRST AMENDMENT CLAIMS

The Old Ways Fellowship ("Old Ways") has several arguments to support its First Amendment Claims. The threshold question for all of its claims is whether there is government action. Government action occurs when the government acts, when a private entity takes on a public function, or when the government is entangled (encourages, participates in, or enables) in private conduct.

Here, Old Ways' claim is against the City Building Authority, which is a part of the City's Municipal Government. Thus, the First Amendment applies because state action is involved.

First Amendment Right to Freedom of Speech

Old Ways has several arguments related to its first amendment right to freedom of speech.

Content-Based Restrictions. Old Ways may also argue that the Policy is an invalid restriction of speech in a public forum. Here, the speech is occurring in the City's Municipal Government Building, which is open to the public, and has permitted public use for speech purposes for many years.

All content-based restrictions on speech conducted in a public or designated public forum are subject to strict scrutiny. Under the strict scrutiny standard, the government has the burden to show that a law is narrowly tailored, using the least restrictive means, to reach a compelling governmental interest. Content-based restrictions on speech arise when the government regulates either subject-matter based speech, or viewpoint based speech. Content-neutral speech conducted in a public or designated public forum must further an important government interest, be narrowly tailored, leave alternatives for speech open, but need not be the least restrictive means available.

Here, Old Ways would first argue that its five-foot diameter symbol of the sun constitutes symbolic speech, as it symbolizes the religion organization's beliefs. It would then argue that the Building Authority's Policy on Seasonal Displays ("Policy") is a content-based regulation because it bars the use of "religious displays and symbols" rather than all symbols and/or displays. If it successfully shows that the Policy is content-based, the city has the burden to establish a compelling interest, and that the Policy is narrowly tailored to reach that interest.

The City will likely argue that the purpose of the policy is not to stop symbolic speech, but to avoid the appearance of government endorsement of religion, which likely qualifies as a compelling interest. It would then argue that completely barring religious symbols and displays is the least restrictive means of accomplishing this goal. Although such an argument may be persuasive in a vacuum, these facts do not indicate that the Policy is the least restrictive means available. Old Ways offered to put up a disclaimer along with its symbol, stating that the sun is not endorsed by the City, but the Building Authority rejected this offer. Such an option restricts Old Ways' speech less, while arguably avoiding government endorsement of religion, but the Building Authority will not allow it. The City's refusal to adopt a less restrictive alternative is a failure to meet the requirements of strict scrutiny.

Prior Restraint. Old Ways can also argue that the Policy is an impermissible prior restraint on speech. Prior restraints are subject to strict scrutiny because they put a barrier on speech before the speech can occur. One such type of prior restraint is a permit that permits speech. To be valid, a permit must further an important government interest, involve little to no discretion by the person or group issuing the permit, there must be clear criteria to obtain the permit, and there must be a procedure in place for timely resolution of the permit and/or an immediate appeal of a decision.

Here, the fact that Old Ways needs a permit to display its sun arguably constitutes a prior restraint. Old Ways would argue that the permit requirement is impermissible because the Building Authority does not have a clear description of what items are and are not permitted to be displayed, beyond a bar on the religious symbols. Because the Building Authority decided to put up a Christmas tree, Old Ways can argue that the standards are not applied in an equal way because certain religious symbols are permitted (the Christmas tree), while other symbols (the sun) are not permitted. Also, Old Ways can point out that the Building Authority uses discretion in determining what to erect in the government building, and that there is no set policy in place for review of a decision rejecting a display. The City may, again, argue that its interest in avoiding the appearance of government endorsement of religion permits the permit requirement, and that there is no discretion involved in the policy because the City completely bars the use of any religious displays and symbols. It will also argue that the Christmas tree does not constitute a religious symbol. However, it is unlikely that the City will prevail in these arguments because there is no set procedure in place for determining who gets a permit, nor an appeals process for rejection of the permit.

Overbreadth. A government regulation of speech is overbroad and invalid where it regulates more speech than intended.

Old Ways may also argue that the Policy is an overbroad regulation of speech. It is unlikely that it will succeed in this argument, however, as the Policy clearly applies to "religious displays and symbols" and there are no facts indicating that the Policy has extended to restrict speech beyond religious speech.

Vagueness. A regulation of speech is vague and invalid where it is unclear what speech is prohibited and what speech is not prohibited.

Old Ways could argue that the Policy is vague because it does not define exactly what constitutes a religious display and symbol. It can argue that because the Christmas tree is not considered a religious symbol, the Policy is vague because Christmas trees are often interpreted to be religious symbols. Such an argument might succeed here. The Building Authority's position is that "courts treat Christmas trees as secular symbols," but the Policy itself does not include a description of what does and does not constitute religious displays or symbols. The lack of specificity in the Policy results in confusion, and thus Old Ways likely will succeed in challenging the Policy on vagueness grounds.

First Amendment Right to Freedom of Religious Expression

Old Ways can also contend that the new policy on seasonal displays unjustifiably infringes upon its freedom to exercise its religion. The general rule regarding freedom of expression is that neutral laws of general applicability that have the effect of infringing on freedom of expression do not violate the right to freedom of expression. However, when a law is not neutral, strict scrutiny applies, requiring the government to show that the law is necessary to further a compelling government interest, and that the law is the least restrictive means possible.

Here, Old Ways would argue that the Policy is not neutral because it bars religious displays and symbols specifically, not just any displays and symbols. Old Ways would also point out that the policy interferes with its ability to spread its Winter Greeting, which is an important aspect of its religion. Thus, strict scrutiny likely applies. As explained above, although the City may have a compelling interest in avoiding government endorsement of religion, the policy is not the least restrictive means available. Thus, Old Ways will likely succeed in challenging the Policy on freedom of expression grounds.

First Amendment Right That the Government Will Not Establish Religion

Old Ways can also contend that the Policy, in practice, establishes religion.

Establishment Clause. The government may not establish a particular religion under the Establishment Clause of the First Amendment. To determine whether government action violates the establishment clause, the court applies what is called the Lemon test, which analyzes the government action under 3 prongs: (1) whether the government action has a secular purpose, (2) whether the action has the effect of promoting or inhibiting a particular religion or religion in general, and (3) whether the action results in excessive entanglement between the government and religion.

Secular Purpose. Here, Old Ways may concede that the purpose of the Policy is secular, and a court would likely agree. The Policy states outright that it is meant to avoid the appearance of government endorsement of religion, and so the first prong does not indicate a violation of the establishment clause.

Effect. Old Ways will argue that the effect of the Policy actually inhibits its religion and promotes a certain religion -- Christianity -- because the Building Authority permitted erection of a Christmas tree but no other religious symbols. The court would likely agree that the effect does promote Christianity and not other religions because the Christmas tree -- and only the Christmas tree -- is displayed. Had the Building Authority permitted other types of symbols along with the Christmas tree, the effect may not be to promote Christianity, but the winter season generally. Thus, this factor supports a finding that the Policy establishes religion.

Entanglement. Finally, Old Ways would argue that the Policy results in excessive entanglement between the government and religion. The City would argue that the Policy seeks to avoid religious involvement completely. Although the Policy appears on its face to attempt to avoid entanglement with religion, because the Building Authority erected the Christmas tree, the City's position is weaker, and the court may find that entanglement has occurred because the Building Authority has permitted an arguably religious symbol, but not others.

Balancing the three factors, it is likely that Old Ways' argument would succeed, and that the court would find that the Policy, as applied by the Building Authority, establishes religion, and is unconstitutional.

QUESTION 5: SELECTED ANSWER B

First Amendment: Freedom of Speech

Old Ways Fellowship will argue that the Building Authority's (BA) "Policy on Seasonal Displays" violates its right to free speech under the First Amendment.

State Action

In order for Old Ways to challenge the Policy under the Constitution there must be state action. Here, BA is the City's agency that issued the policy restricting religious displays and symbols from government property. Thus, since BA is a branch of the City, there is state action.

Content-Based vs. Content-Neutral

Old Ways' success under the First Amendment Free speech clause will depend on whether the Policy is found to be content-based or content-neutral. Here, BA adopted the Policy on Seasonal Displays which expressly prohibits "religious" displays and symbols on government property but does not appear to apply to non-religious displays. Old Ways will argue that the policy does not restrict groups or organizations from displaying other forms of artwork or paintings but directly is singling out religious displays and other secular symbols. Thus, the policy will likely be found to be content-based.

City may try and argue that the Policy does not single out a particular religion and thus it should be found to be content neutral but this is a weaker argument since religious content, by itself, is a category of speech and thus the policy will likely be found to focus on this content.

Strict Scrutiny

Laws that are content-based and restrict speech must pass strict scrutiny. The government bears the burden of showing that the law or statute is necessary to achieve a compelling state interest with no less discriminatory alternatives.

City/BA will claim that the policy is designed to prohibit the appearance of government endorsement of religion. City will further attempt to show that certain symbols are clearly religiously oriented and that simply by their presence in the Municipal building, this gives off the impression that the City endorses the religions associated with those symbols or displays. The prevention of endorsement of religion is likely a compelling interest since the First Amendment does not permit the government to favor one religion over another.

The weakness in City's arguments is that the law does not appear to be necessary, even if the City has a compelling interest in preventing the appearance of religious endorsement. Old Ways will argue that the City has a long history of allowing it to display its Winter Solstice display along with a variety of other public and private speakers and displays in the lobby. Old Ways will claim that the city is randomly choosing to single out religious displays by completely preventing them in government buildings via its new Policy. The law is likely not necessary to achieve the City's interest here.

As Old Ways will point out, there are less discriminatory alternatives in achieving the City's desired purpose. Old Ways offered to put up a disclaimer sign explaining that the Winter Solstice greeting is not endorsed by City. Presumably people that take the time to observe the displays in the Municipal building would also notice the disclaimer assuming it was prominently displayed beside the various displays. This would be sufficient to allow Old Ways to continue its time-honored tradition of wishing people a Happy Winter Solstice through its display while not suggesting that City endorses Old Ways religious beliefs. City could also hand out pamphlets at the entrances to government buildings describing its policy of allowing the displays and putting the disclaimer there as well.

Thus, as strict scrutiny is a difficult standard to meet, it appears that BA will have a difficult time showing the policy is necessary when there are less discriminatory alternatives present. The law should be struck down as unconstitutional.

Time, Manner, Place

Even if the court were to find that the BA Policy is not content-based but rather is content-neutral because it does not single out any particular religion and appears to apply to all religions equally, Old Ways will argue that it is still an invalid time, place and manner regulation.

Time, manner and place regulations are permitted for content neutral and viewpoint neutral regulations depending on the type of location where the speech is being regulated. Traditionally, public forums are those that have historically been open to the public such as sidewalks and parks, while designated or limited public forums are those that the government has chosen to hold open to public speech but can close at any time. Public forums and designated/limited public forums must meet intermediate scrutiny, such that the law is substantially related to an important government and there must be other nondiscriminatory alternatives available.

Here, the Policy is affecting government buildings, including the lobby of the Municipal building. A lobby of a government building would not be a public forum but rather a designated public forum since it appears that City has for some time chosen to allow various organizations to put their displays and speakers in the lobby of the Municipal building. City could certainly close off the lobby to such displays if it wanted to.

Old Ways will argue that, while City may have an important interest, even a compelling interest as discussed above, in preventing the appearance of government endorsed religion, the Policy is simply not substantially related to this interest. Furthermore City will have the burden of demonstrating the substantial relation. City will likely claim that the law is substantially related because it singles out displays from buildings that are government owned and that the Policy only focuses on the interior of government buildings. City will claim that there are other nondiscriminatory alternatives such as Old Ways displaying its displays outside the buildings or on the plazas in front of the building. This argument will likely fail however, because while Old Ways may indeed have other options for displaying its Winter Solstice display, it cannot join the other displays that are permitted to be inside the Municipal building and this particular location is where people have come to expect to see the Winter Solstice display each year.

Therefore, because the Policy still singles out only religious displays from government buildings, the City may have a difficult time prevailing on a time manner place argument since there are other less discriminatory options that would allow Old Ways to actually continue to display the displays inside the building while notifying viewers that there is no endorsement by City of any particular religion.

Symbolic Speech

Old Ways will argue that the policy impermissibly regulates symbolic speech. Symbolic speech can be regulated if it is done in a way that is unrelated to the suppression of speech and if there are other less discriminatory alternatives.

City will argue that by adopting the Policy it was not attempting to regulate Old Ways' right to free speech through the Winter Solstice displays. While there may be other alternatives, as previously mentioned, for Old Ways to continue this form of symbolic expression, City will likely lose on the ground that the Policy was related to the suppression of speech. The Policy directly bans symbols and displays with religious content. Thus, it would appear that the BA, in considering the adoption of the Policy, had a direct motive to regulate what types of displays would and would not be allowed.

Furthermore, Old Ways will argue that City continues to allow the display of Christmas trees in the buildings and that Christmas trees are typically associated with a religious holiday. Thus the policy may be found to impermissibly regulate only certain religious symbolic speech while other groups attempting to display Christmas displays will be allowed.

Since Old Ways' displays are not permitted in the buildings and the policy directly and expressly provides for this, the law will likely be found to be an unconstitutional restriction of symbolic speech.

Vagueness and Overbreadth

Old Ways may bring a vagueness or overbreadth challenge to the Policy. Laws are vague if one cannot tell what speech is banned and what is permitted. Overbreadth laws are those that impermissibly burden more speech than is allowed.

Here, the Policy could be struck down as vague because it does not define what exactly constitutes religious displays; thus it is insufficient to put one on notice as to whether its display is or is not affected by the policy. Furthermore, the policy may be overbroad in that it bans all symbols and displays, even if they do not have any religious meaning associated with them. Old Ways may or may not succeed on these grounds.

Free Exercise of Religion

The free exercise clause of the Constitution prohibits the government from preventing one's free exercise of his or her religion. Laws of general applicability are permissible while laws that target a specific religion must meet strict scrutiny.

Here, the Policy, while it does apply to all religious displays and symbols, does not appear to single out any particular religion. Nor is there any evidence of BA singling out Old Ways' particular religious beliefs as a motive for adopting the law. Thus, Old Ways would have a better likelihood of success challenging the policy under the Establishment clause.

Establishment Clause

Old Ways will argue that the Policy respects an establishment of religion since the City is allowed to display Christmas trees while other religious displays and symbols are banned. The Establishment clause prohibits the government from respecting the establishment of a religion. If a law has a secular purpose on its face, it must meet strict scrutiny. Laws that are not secular on their face must pass the three part lemon test.

First the law must have a nonsecular purpose. Here, the law bans all religious displays and symbols. If the court finds that this is a secular purpose because it specifically targets religious displays, then this requirement will fail.

Second, the law must neither advance nor inhibit religion. The law appears not to advance religion since it bans displays to prevent government endorsement of religion so this requirement is satisfied.

Third, the law must lead to no excessive government entanglement with religion. Here, the problem is that the City policy is banning Old Ways displays while allowing the erection of a Christmas tree in the same space as where Old Ways displays were permitted. Thus, the court may find that the policy impermissibly entangles the government with religion if it finds that the City is really making space for its own preferred religious displays while forcing out other displays such as Old Ways that it finds unattractive or not interesting.

Thus, Old Ways may have a colorable claim under the Establishment Clause.

Question 6

Angela hired Mark, a real estate broker, to help her find a house to buy.

A week later, Mark contacted Angela and told her that he had found the perfect house for her. She asked him what he knew about the house. He said that the house had been owned for some years by Carol, who had kept it in pristine condition. When she visited the house, Angela noticed what appeared to be animal droppings on the deck. Carol assured her that they were only bird droppings, had never appeared previously, and would be removed before closing. Carol added that she never had any problem with any kind of "pests." Angela made an offer of $500,000 for the house, and Carol accepted.

After closing, Angela spent $10,000 to move her household goods to the house. A few weeks after moving into the house, Angela made several discoveries. First, the house suffered from a seasonal infestation of bats, which urinated and defecated on the deck. Second, Carol was in fact Mark's cousin, had owned the house for about a year, and had been desperate to sell it because of the bats. Mark was aware of all of these facts.

After the sale, Mark evenly split the proceeds with Carol and invested his $250,000 in stocks that are now worth $750,000.

At trial, Angela has established that Mark and Carol are liable to her in tort and contract.

1. What remedy or remedies may Angela obtain against Carol? Discuss.

2. What remedy or remedies may Angela obtain against Mark? Discuss.

QUESTION 6: SELECTED ANSWER A

1. Angela v. Carol

Rescission

Angela (A) may seek to have the contract with Carol (C) for the sale of the house rescinded. There must be grounds for the rescission and no defenses preventing it. A asked C about animal droppings she saw on the back deck and C assured A that they were only bird droppings and had never appeared previously. C then added, on her own, that she never had any problem with pests. These statements amount to a material misrepresentation of fact by C to A. A material misrepresentation is grounds for rescission if the seller made a misrepresentation of a fact that a reasonable buyer would have relied on and the buyer did in fact rely on the statements. While generally the doctrine of caveat emptor applies to omissions, there is implied in every land contract a duty not to make material misrepresentations. Generally the failure to mention a material fact is not actionable, though in some instances a court may hold the seller liable for known latent defects. However, here, C affirmatively represented, of her own accord, the fact that there were no problems with pests. And C also misrepresented the fact that the droppings were from bats that seasonally infest the house. These assurances made by C to A are of the type reasonably relied on by a buyer, since a buyer can't inspect a house for a whole year, she must rely on the seller's representation regarding seasonal conditions. Here, A did in fact rely on the misrepresentation. Thus, A has grounds for rescission.

C may try to bring the defenses of laches or unclean hands, however, A did nothing wrong to make her hands unclean and she discovered the infestation within weeks of the sale. This short period of time did not unfairly prejudice C so laches does not apply either.

Compensatory Damages

Compensatory damages aim to make the plaintiff whole, to put them in the position they would have been in had the contract been fully and properly performed. Here, A expected to own a house free of infestation. With the contract rescission, A has a right to the return of the price paid for the house plus any consequential and incidental damages. Consequential damages are those damages specific to the plaintiff that were foreseeable at the time the contract was entered. Incidental costs are those associated with dealing with the breach. Here, A is entitled to a return of the purchase price ($500,000) plus the costs associated with moving her household goods into the house since it was foreseeable at the time of contract that she would need to move her items ($10,000) plus any other incidental damages incurred in dealing with the breach (for instance, moving out costs or protecting her personal property from damage from the bats).

Punitive Damages

Punitive damages are not awarded in contracts claims. However, C's misrepresentations likely raise to the level of fraud and are thus actionable under tort law. In that case, C may be liable for penal damages for fraud. See discussion below regarding Mark's liability for penal damages.

Restitutionary Damages

Alternatively, A may recover restitutionary damages from C. Restitutionary damages seek to prevent the defendant from being unjustly enriched. The plaintiff may recover the reasonable value of the benefit received by the defendant. Here, C was unjustly enriched when she received the full contract price of $500,000 for a house she knew to be seasonally infested with bats. A could recover the benefit to C of the contract price. However, the house was likely worth something, just not the full contract price. So any restitutionary recovery will likely look at the fair market value of the house as is (with infestation) and award A the difference between the contract price and the fair market value.

Note that A may not recover both compensatory and restitutionary damages and thus will likely elect compensatory as the larger amount of damages.

Constructive Trust / Equitable Lien

A may get a constructive trust or an equitable lien over the compensatory or restitutionary money damages due to her. (See rules below)

2. Angela v. Mark

Angela may have entered into a contract with Mark (M) for his brokerage services but more likely he was held liable in tort for fraud. Fraud is the intentional misrepresentation of a past or present fact, made with the intent that the other rely on it and the other does reasonably rely. M was C's cousin, he knew of the bat infestation and that C was desperate to sell the house. He told A that the house was in pristine condition and he stood by while C represented that the house was free of any infestation. M also received half the proceeds from the house.

Compensatory Damages

See rule above. A may recover the full cost of the house as well as the cost of moving in ($510,000), which represents the position she would have been in if the tort had not occurred. If M had not committed a fraud and induced A to purchase the house, she would not have spent the money to purchase and move in to the bat infested house.

Punitive Damages

If a defendant acts wantonly, willfully or maliciously, the plaintiff may also recover punitive damages as long as she recovers either compensatory or nominal damages as well (and sometimes restitutionary). Punitive damages seek to punish the defendant for his willful wrongdoing. Here, M was related to C and knew of the poor condition of the house. He knew that the house was infested and that C was desperate to sell because of the bats. This knowledge made M's actions in showing the house to A, representing that it was in pristine condition and not warning A of the bats willful. Thus, A will likely recover punitive damages for M's willful conduct.

Note: As mentioned above, C may also be liable for fraud and her active misrepresentations could also be found to be willful and malicious. Thus, A may also recover punitive damages from C in connection with the compensatory or restitutionary damages owed by C.

Restitutionary Damages

See rule above. M has been unjustly enriched since he received half the proceeds from the sale to A which was based on his fraud. He may have also received a broker's fee, also an unjust enrichment. A is entitled to the reasonable value of this benefit. Here, M received a $250,000 benefit. Thus, A may recover $250,000.

Constructive Trust / Equitable Lien

A constructive trust is a court order that the defendant hold the property in trust for the benefit of the plaintiff and return the property to the plaintiff, along with any enhanced value. If the property is no longer available but may be traced to another form, as long as it can be traced with certainty, the plaintiff may still recover the value of the property by tracing. Here, A may seek a constructive trust on M's $250,000. M invested the money in stocks that are now worth $750,000. Because the original $250,000 can be clearly traced to the stocks, A may recover the full, enhanced value of the property. Thus A is entitled to the stocks which are now worth $750,000.

An equitable lien is a court-imposed security interest in the property which must be sold and the proceeds returned to the plaintiff. If the sale results in less money than is owed, the plaintiff may get a deficiency judgment and a lien on the defendant's other property to secure that judgment. However, the plaintiff may not recover any enhanced value in the property. Tracing may also be used to ensure return of the property. Here, A could get an equitable lien on the stocks (traceable from the money M received) and force a sale of the stocks in order to receive the $250,000 of restitutionary damages she is owed. She would not be entitled to the full $750,000 under an equitable lien.

Thus, A will seem a constructive trust in order to recover the restitutionary damages owed to her.

QUESTION 6: SELECTED ANSWER B

1. Angela's remedies against Carol.

The issue is to what remedies Angela is entitled to obtain against Carol for Carol's liability in tort and contract.

In contract
Damages for breach of contract can either be legal or equitable.

Legal Remedies

Damages

The typical measure of damages in contract is the expectation measure. That is, the non-breaching party to a contract is entitled to be put in the same position that she would have been in had the other party not breached the contract. Here, at the end of the contract, Angela expected to be in possession of a house that was in "pristine condition" that did not have a bat infestation.

Presumably, the seasonal bat infestation reduced the market value of the house and Angela would not have paid $500,000 for the house had she known of it. Therefore, in order to protect Angela's expectation, she is entitled to receive the difference between $500,000 contract price and the market value of the house at the time of closing.

Angela is not entitled to her $10,000 of moving expenses as damages because she would have had to spend that amount if the house was in the condition she expected it to be, regardless of the bats.

Finally, Angela has not suffered any consequential damages from the purchase of the house (losses that are foreseeable at the time of contract) and punitive damages are not recoverable in contract.

Restitution

Angela may also recover on a restitution theory. Restitution is a remedy that is used to avoid unjust enrichment from a party's wrongdoing. Here, due to Carol's misrepresentations, she was able to sell the house at a price above its market value. Therefore, Angela may recover the difference in the contract price and the fair market value of the house at the time of closing.

Again, Angela is not entitled to the $10,000 in moving expenses in restitution because those moving expenses were paid to a mover, not to Carol.

Equitable Remedies

Rescission

Rescission of a contract is an equitable remedy whereby the contract is rescinded as if it never happened. Essentially, the party seeking rescission must argue that the contract was never formed because there was no meeting of the minds. If the contract here is rescinded, Angela would receive her $500,000 purchase price while Carol would be put back in possession of the house. Grounds for rescission include: mistake and misrepresentation.

There are two types of mistake: Mutual Mistake and Unilateral Mistake. Mutual mistake exists where both parties to a contract are mistaken as to a fact that substantially affects the basis of their bargain. Here, Carol was not mistaken about any facts with regard to the contract--she knew of the bat infestation and its effects.

Angela will be able to successfully argue unilateral mistake. Unilateral mistake is not typically a grounds for rescission. However, when the non-mistaken party knows of the mistake of the other party and proceeds with knowledge in the face of that mistake, the mistaken party may rescind the contract. Here, because Angela did not know of the bat infestation, and Carol both knew of the infestation and knew that Angela did not know of it, unilateral mistake is applicable and Angela may rescind on that ground.

In addition to the ground of unilateral mistake, Angela may rescind on grounds of misrepresentation. Misrepresentation occurs when a party makes a material misrepresentation, with the intent that the other party rely on the statement, the reliance is justified, the other party does indeed rely on the statement and that party suffers damage. Here, Carol misrepresented that she had never seen the droppings before and that they were bird droppings. She intended for Angela to rely on the statement and Angela did indeed rely on the statement and suffer damages. The only issue is whether Angela's reliance was justified. Considering that Mark said that Carol kept the home pristine and Angela was assured by Carol, the homeowner, regarding the condition of the house, Angela's reliance was likely justified. Carol may be able to argue that Angela should have hired an independent appraiser of the house instead of relying on her statement, but this argument will fail because Angela's reliance was justified given Mark's corroboration of the condition of the house.

Therefore, the equitable remedy of rescission is warranted on grounds of unilateral mistake and misrepresentation and Angela should be entitled to her $500,000, and the house will be returned to Carol.

<u>In Tort</u>

Legal Remedies

Damages

Angela may sue Carol for damages in the amount that Carol's misrepresentation cost her. Therefore, she should be able to recover the amount that will be required to fix the bat infestation and any damage already caused by the bats.

In addition, Angela may be able to recover punitive damages from Carol because of Carol's outrageous lies and conduct. Not only did Carol lie about the droppings and that she had never seen them before, she had been desperate to sell the house and was Mark's cousin, with whom she perpetrated a fraud on Angela. Typically, punitive damages are limited to a cap of less than ten times the actual damages.

Equitable Remedies

Constructive Trust

A constructive trust is a restitutionary equitable remedy. If a constructive trust is imposed, the defendant must return the property to the plaintiff. A constructive trust will be imposed when 1) the defendant holds title to property, 2) title was acquired by the defendant's wrongful conduct, and 3) retention of the property would result in the unjust enrichment of the defendant. Typically, the plaintiff will pursue a constructive trust when the value of the property increases while the defendant has held the property.

Here, Carol holds the proceeds from the sale, she acquired it with wrongful conduct as discussed above, and retention of the proceeds would result in unjust enrichment. However, the legal remedies described above are adequate to remedy Angela's harm. Therefore, the court should not grant this remedy.

Equitable Lien

An equitable lien is also a restitutionary equitable remedy. If an equitable lien is imposed, the plaintiff will acquire a security interest in the property and the property will be subject to an immediate court ordered sale, and the plaintiff will be entitled to the proceeds. An equitable lien will be granted upon the same conditions as a constructive trust.

Angela will be able to show the conditions for imposition of an equitable lien have been met. However, the legal remedies described above are adequate to remedy Angela's harm. Therefore, the court should not grant this remedy.

2. Angela's remedies against Mark.

Equitable Remedies

Constructive Trust

The requirements of a constructive trust are listed above. Because the source of the funds used to purchase the stock is directly traceable to his unjust enrichment from the transaction, Angela will be able to force Mark to turn over the stock to her in a constructive trust. She will be entitled to keep the entire value of the stock.

Equitable Lien

Angela will be able to show she is entitled to an equitable lien. The court will trace the proceeds that Mark used to purchase the stock to his unjust enrichment from his involvement in the transaction, and Angela will be granted a security interest in the property. Then, the stock will be subject to sale and Angela will be entitled to receive Mark's $250,000.

Legal Remedies

Replevin-

Damages-